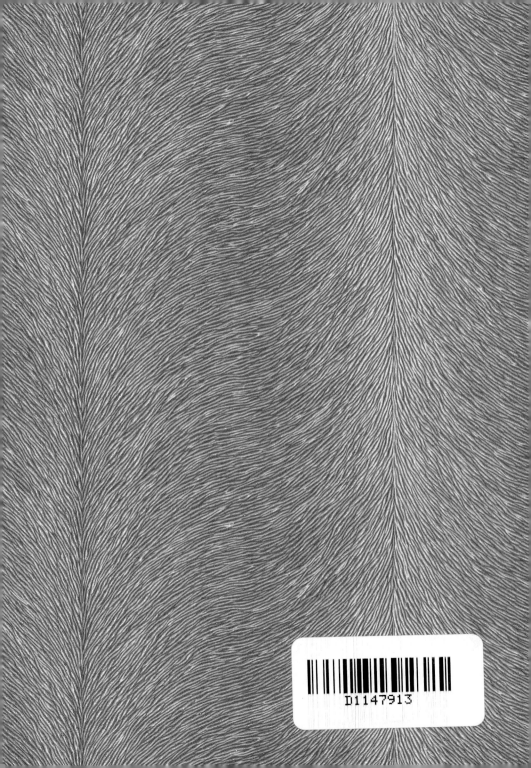

Third Age Press

**ON THE TIP
OF YOUR TONGUE**

YOUR MEMORY IN LATER LIFE

ON
THE TIP
OF
YOUR
TONGUE

YOUR
MEMORY
IN
LATER LIFE

DR
H B GIBSON

Designed and illustrated by Rufus Segar

x

Third Age Press

London
1995

ISBN 1 898576 05 X

First edition.
Third Age Press Ltd, 1995
Third Age Press, 6 Parkside Gardens
London, SW19 5EY

Editor Dianne Norton

Set on a Macintosh in Saltwood
Hythe, Kent by the MacSegar Press, Sandacre

Printed and bound in Great Britain
by Bell & Bain Limited, Glasgow

Dedication

In writing this book I have been particularly indebted to Carol Graham. Not only has she read the whole manuscript and advised on stylistic presentation, but the content of it owes much to our discussions.

ABOUT THE ILLUSTRATOR

Rufus Segar is a designer and an illustrator. For 30 years under *The Economist* umbrella he aspired to be a good typographer and delighted in complicated graphs and diagrams for economic texts. For most of that time he was freelance, he had been employed by publishers and agencies in his 20s. He did the covers once a month for *Anarchy* throughout the 60s.

The computer arrived in 1984 and rendered typography and chart making witless and obsolete. He left London for Hythe in Kent five years ago and has happily become a topographer. Books to his credit include:

Cockney Alphabet R Segar   London: Max Parrish. 1965

A LOST MASTERPIECE OF CARTOGRAPHIC DIAGRAMS:

The Atlas of Europe   R C Croucher & M C MacDonald (Eds)
        Edinburgh and London:
        John Bartholomew and Frederick Warne. 1974

COMIC ILLUSTRATIONS FOR SERIOUS BOOKS:

In *The Economist* Pocket Books series:

The Economist Pocket Style Book   1986

Pocket Lawyer   S Berwin 1987

Pocket Taxpayer   B Sabine 1987

Pocket Guide to Business Taxes   B Sabine 1988

SERIOUS TOPOGRAPHIC DRAWINGS WITH COMIC TOUCHES:

Remember Hythe: The High Street: 1902 – 1992
        Hythe, Kent: MacSegar Press. 1992 (a trove and still in print)

Remember St Martin's Cheriton: 1993

Remember St Peter and St Paul Saltwood, Hythe: 1994 (3 parts)

Remember the Watermill at Hythe   Hythe Imperial Hotel: 1994

ALL THESE THREE ABOVE SIMPLY TO FUND THE FABRIC

The Town Hall of Hythe, One of the Cinque Ports   D Rayner. 1994
        Hythe Civic Society: which has got him to illustrate:

Our Time in Hythe: Review 1945 – 1995   G Roberts (Ed)
        Hythe, Kent: Hythe Civic Society. 1995

ABOUT THE AUTHOR

Dr H B Gibson is currently Honorary Senior Research Fellow at the University of Hertfordshire where he was Head of the Department of Psychology from 1970 to 1976. His 50-year teaching career has spanned Criminology, Clinical Psychology and Hypnosis. The latter interest has led him into service as an Expert Witness in criminal and civil court cases. For the past 10 years he has taken an active interest in matters gerontological. He is a tutor and active member of the University of the Third Age in Cambridge and lectures and writes on a broad sweep of Third Age issues.

He has written prolifically over the years on a wide range of topics including contributions to journals of a humanist, sceptical and anarchist orientation. Notable publications include:

Psychology, Pain and Anaesthesia H B Gibson (Ed)
        London: Chapman Hall. 1993
Emotional and sexual adjustment in later life.
In *Ageing, Independence and the Life Course*
        (Eds. S Arber & M Evandrou) London:
        Jessica Kingsley Publications. 1993
Love, Sex and Power in Later Life
        London: Freedom Press. 1992
The Emotional and Sexual Lives of Older People:
A Manual for Professionals
        London: Chapman & Hall. 1991
The Nature of Hypnosis. In E Karas (Ed)
Current Issues in Clinical Psychology
        New York: Plenum Publishing Co. 1987
Pain and its Conquest
        London: Peter Owen Ltd. 1982
Hans Eysenck: The Man and His Work
        London: Peter Owen Ltd. 1981

CONTENTS

INTRODUCTION

This book is addressed to the vast majority of people who, being mentally and physically healthy, are entering what has come to be called the Third Age, an age that can be as happy and satisfying as any other period of life.

As people approach old age many expect to suffer from forgetfulness and a general deterioration of their mental ability. Such expectation is unjustified, and this book aims to make it clear that there is no valid reason to expect any such thing. Certainly changes take place, just as significant developments have been taking place throughout your life, but if you understand the nature of these changes and know how to adapt to them, they should not incommode you. Considerable progress has been made recently in scientific research into the processes of ageing, and I hope to acquaint you with the latest findings written in plain English and not scientific jargon.

Chapter 1 explains the nature of memory, and how it is best understood as a record of past events that is constantly being modified by your on-going experience. Forgetting is due to two things: the impression not being well recorded in the first place, and an inability to retrieve what is stored in the memory-bank because of various complex factors. There is little evidence that forgetting is due to any 'fading' of a memory in the way that writing may fade from paper.

Nine of the more common myths about memory and their origins are discussed in **Chapter 2**. Most people have grown up with these myths which tend to undermine their faith in their own ability to learn new things in later life, and so they mistrust their own abilities.

In other words, they may become a self-fulfilling prophesy. The fact that many people expect to 'lose their memory' in later life is due to a number of different things.

First, there are the diseases of old age that injure the brain and seriously impair the sufferers' mental ability, but these diseases affect only a small minority of people in later life. They are not the result of being old any more than chicken-pox is the result of being young! Second, everyone recognizes that their physical powers will lessen as they grow older, beginning in our 20s, but it is a mistake to assume that mental ability deteriorates also. It is understandable that tradition holds that this is so, for in earlier times even to be middle-aged was, for many people, to suffer from considerable handicap. Just think what it would be like to suffer from weak eyesight before the days of the wide availability of spectacles – you might as well have been illiterate. In modern times the wearing of spectacles is taken for granted, yet defective hearing is almost as common as defective eyesight in later life, but the wearing of hearing aids is less usual, and partial deafness tends to give the impression that a person is 'slow on the uptake'. Such disability is often mistakenly attributed to a supposed age-related deterioration of mental ability.

Most of the myths discussed are of very ancient lineage, and have only been firmly exploded by modern research, but because they form part of the well-established folklore of our society, they sometimes affect even professional people. We still have GPs who are apt to treat their older patients as though they are a bit doddery simply because of their age, and there are young psychologists and social workers who cannot accept the fact that some of their older clients are a lot brighter than they are.

In some chapters you will find practical exercises which should be fun as well as enlightening. Please attempt at least some of them, for not only will they demonstrate to you techniques for efficient learning and overcoming blockages of memory, but they will enable you to learn more about yourself. People vary very much as to the type of learning techniques that suit them best, some finding visual imagery most helpful, and others having good verbal ability. All you need for these exercises is a supply of blank paper.

Chapter 3 describes the normal changes that take place with ageing in the processes of learning and memory, and explains why they occur. The old idea was that the brain 'deteriorates' with ageing just as the muscles become less powerful, but modern research has challenged this over-simple idea. The confusion that arises through mistaking physical for mental changes is discussed at some length, and practical advice is given as to how to adapt to change and over-come some of the common complaints about forgetting, which are due to the developments of later life.

Topics such as remembering to do things in the future, and absent-mindedness receive special consideration in **Chapter 3**. Such problems are not necessarily peculiar to older people, but may occur at any age when the memory is under special stress. Being unable to recall a name or a word that is usually quite familiar to you, is known as the tip-of-the-tongue (TOT) experience, and the whole of **Chapter 4** is devoted to it. A study of this phenomenon will teach you a lot about the mechanisms of memory, and I shall introduce you to several techniques for breaking such blockages of memory.

Chapter 5 is concerned with mnemonics, the well-known gimmicks for learning and memorizing that can be traced back to the classical times of Greece and Rome. While some of them are useful in certain circumstances, too much should not be expected of them in daily life. They figure largely in the books on memory that are written for schoolchildren and students who need to do a great deal of cramming for examinations, but while you should know about them, you should pick and choose among them as to what will be useful to you.

Practical work in improving memory is presented in **Chapter 6**, and it is demonstrated what can be achieved by certain methods, and why some other methods are probably useless. Although a great deal of work on improving memory in psychological laboratories has been done in the past, the scientific study of memory improvement in daily life has received serious attention only comparatively recently. One of the difficulties in such work is to devise the means of assessing how good people's memory is before the memory training course is given, in order to re-assess it after. Only thus can it be determined how effective the training has been. Measurement is possible by asking people to complete questionnaire forms of self-assessment concerning their experience in daily life.

It has become apparent that it is not very meaningful to refer to 'a bad memory', for some people may be very forgetful of other people's names, but have no difficulty in remembering where everything is located in the house, while with other people it is the exact reverse. A questionnaire concerning 10 areas of possible forgetfulness is presented, and if you wish to answer this yourself, you may compare your own ratings with those of a group of people over the age of 60 whom I have tested.

In **Chapter 7** the characteristics of the people in later life whom I call 'task-oriented' are contrasted with those of people I refer to as 'lotos-eaters'. You may like to consider which type you resemble most closely. Your personal type may have a lot to do with how you regard mental ability in later life. Structured reminiscence, as suggested by Eric Midwinter in *A Voyage of Rediscovery: a guide to writing your life story*, is recommended as a means of consolidating the material in your memory bank. Such an exercise should be a pleasure in itself as well as teaching you something about how your memory works. My book aims to explain the mechanisms of memory, and with such an understanding you will be in a better position to deal with whatever problems confront you in later life.

The purpose of the final chapter is to clarify matters concerning the diseases and derangements of memory that affect a minority of older people, and to make it quite clear that these are not the results of ageing as such. Many people are fearful, quite unnecessarily, of what lies ahead of them. The best way of dispelling a threatening bogy is to face it squarely.

This book is based not only on my acquaintance with modern scientific research, but upon experience of conducting seminars with groups of people in the Third Age, and discussions with them of the problems of everyday life relating to learning and memory. As far as I know, this book is unique; although there are many other books, both good and bad, on the subject of memory, no other book is devoted exclusively to memory in later life.

1

WHAT IS MEMORY ?

Memory refers to the activity of storing and retrieving information. Memory is a process – just like your digestion. Just as the activity of digesting proceeds in your stomach, and involves several organs, so remembering proceeds in your brain, which is indeed a collection of related systems that may act separately but in harmony with one another. There is no one part of the brain that is specially concerned with memory.

What has always puzzled people is that they have expected the brain to contain something like graven wax tablets, or written papers, or a gramophone record and a film, or in modern times a videotape, upon which all our past experience is indelibly recorded – and in reality there is nothing like that at all. Remembering is a reconstructive process – each time you remember you re-create, and your reconstructions are not always precisely the same.

It's not necessary to give a firm definition of memory here – by the time you have read this book and tried out some of the suggestions in it you should have a very good grasp of the nature of memory, and having such an understanding you will be able to remember much more efficiently in your daily life.

It would perhaps be better to refer to 'memories' in the plural, for remembering is not a single activity. Any technical terms, such as 'semantic memory' or 'iconic memory', will be explained in commonsense language.

THE FOUR MEMORY SYSTEMS

First, consider the different systems that are involved in memory, and it is convenient to divide them into four: sensory memory, short-term memory, long-term memory, and the retrieval system.

Sensory memory. You see a flash of lightning – you hear a mouse squeak – you feel the prick of a thorn. The stimulus is over in a fraction of a second, but it lingers in the sensory memory long enough for you to consider the jagged shape of the lightning flash, to wonder whether it really was a mouse – or the squeak of a door? You consider the severity of the prick – was it just a puncture or a long scratch? Sensory experiences leave memories that last long enough for you to assess them.

Short-term memory. This is best considered in terms of being told a telephone number by Directory Inquiries. You know from experience that the number will soon fade from your memory unless you write it down. Where is the paper and pencil? You go on repeating 1243 61752 - 1243 61752 - 1243 61752, over and over again to yourself to keep the number active in your memory until you have found the memo pad. Information in the short-term memory system is very vulnerable to distraction. Have you ever experienced the following? You look up a telephone number in the directory and are about to dial it when someone asks you a question: 'Are you going to see the

Jacksons today?' You answer the question and find that by briefly shifting your attention the number has gone out of your short-term memory and you have to look it up again. What goes into your short-term memory depends, of course, on what you see, hear, feel, etc. That is, it depends on your sensory memory. If you want to remember information, to store it so that it is there to be retrieved after a long lapse of time, it has to be transferred to the long-term memory. I am going to use the term 'memory-bank' to refer to information that is stored away.

Long-term memory. In order to transfer information from the short-term to the long-term memory, you have to work on it. It will not go there automatically – it will be wiped clean off the slate, as it were, in your short-term memory. This wiping away from the short-term memory is entirely necessary as otherwise the system would become cluttered up with totally unnecessary bits of information. The metaphor of a slate on which information is temporarily stored is a good one. Working on the information that is temporarily in the short-term memory consists of the activity of attaching it to 'pegs', as it were, that are already present in the long-term memory. You can think of 'pegging' it there or of putting it into pre-existent 'files' or 'pigeon-holes', and in order to do that it has to be classified and put in the right place, or you will never be able to retrieve it.

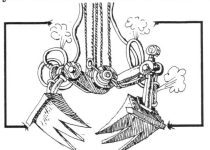

Retrieval. Now we come to the question of retrieval. It would be useless to have information in the memory-bank if you could not retrieve it when required, and this is the trouble with all of us. We have a lot stored away that we simply cannot get at, and that is what constitutes most of our 'forgetting' which will be discussed later.

It will be as well to put all the above information into a simple diagram in order to discuss it further.

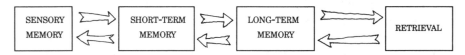

Obviously there are no boxes , or even anatomically separate areas in the brain where all this goes on. It is entirely a matter of convenience to represent the processes in this manner. You will note that not only does information go from the short-term memory into the long-term memory as represented by the arrow, but there is a flow of information in the reverse direction also. This is common sense, for how otherwise could the sounds we hear from the telephone receiver be perceived as the words 'Oh double-two oh . . . etc' unless the information about the English language, which is stored in the long-term memory, were fed back? If the operator spoke in Swahili all you would have would be a series of incomprehensible noises, unless of course, a knowledge of Swahili is also stored in your long-term memory-bank.

FORGETTING

Not all forgetting is due to a failure in the retrieval process. Suppose you ask me to tell you the date of the death of the prime minister Lloyd George, and I cannot tell you. Have I forgotten it? There are several alternative possibilities:

(a) 'I never heard it, or read it, so it never entered my memory system.'

(b) 'I believe that I was told it (or read it in a newspaper) at the time, but I was so little interested that it never got transferred to my long-term memory-bank.'

(c) 'I think I remembered it for a while, and if so, it must have been in my memory-bank, but I probably did not classify it very well, so I really can't retrieve it.'

(d) 'I have an idea that it was in 1945, but such a lot happened then that I really can't be sure as to the date. I think it was early in the year, March, April or May.'

(e) 'I know it perfectly well – it was on the 26th of the month, which is my birthday, but I can't remember the month or the year at the moment. It is on the tip of my tongue, but I am blocking on it – I find it most frustrating.'

Above are several reasons for not knowing a piece of information – that you never encountered it in the first place, that you did come across it but never registered it at all in your long-term memory – that it was registered, but not properly in the correct 'pigeonhole' and is therefore difficult to retrieve – that you know it is there but cannot retrieve it at the moment. The last of these instances of failing to retrieve information, the tip-of-the-tongue phenomenon, is so interesting that a special chapter is devoted to it later on.

REASONS FOR FORGETTING
There are several theories of forgetting, and there is some degree of controversy among psychologists about it. I think I have shown above that memory is not an all-or-none process, and so, when we forget there may be more than one process at work. Here are several of the main theories of forgetting:

 **Decay.** This is the oldest theory of forgetting and is probably the idea that most people have. It goes along with the idea that a memory of something is like a figure engraved on a wax tablet, and with time it will simply decay and become less and less distinct. Something like this does

probably happen in the short-term memory, as the contents disappear so quickly, but there is little evidence that there is any such decay in the memory-bank of the long-term memory.

 **New information distorting old.** This is one of the most difficult concepts to accept, because people do not like to admit to themselves that some – and perhaps a lot – of what they remember never really happened quite the way they remember. Having accepted it myself, I fully realize that what I remember of the past this month may not be precisely the same as the version I will remember next month! It will all depend on what happens to me in the intervening period. There is plenty of evidence for this, a lot of it coming from the extensive studies of eyewitness testimony to the courts.

It is perfectly possible to alter a witness' memory by means of leading questions and make him forget important evidence. Thus if a witness is asked, 'At about what speed did the blue car pass you when it hit Mr Jones?' he is being fed information that the car actually touched the pedestrian and this may distort his previous (and correct) memory that it really just missed him. This is an old trick used by barristers, and judges have to be on the lookout for such leading questions which may distort witness' memory.

If you have ever listened to a husband and wife jointly trying to tell you about an incident that happened to them long ago, you may have had ample evidence of forgetting due to distortion of memory. With the best will in the world, they tell different stories, occasionally correcting one another. 'No, darling, that was at Exeter the year before.' 'But we hadn't got the Morris Estate car then – we had the old Ford.' 'Look, my love, I couldn't have gone to the funeral in my mini. I'd stopped wearing it years before!'

Interference. This is rather like distortion, but it is more a case of one memory actually cancelling out another memory, and leaving nothing in its place, not even memory for the new information. Thus if you go to a foreign language class, and the teacher foolishly gives you a vocabulary list that is far too long, while you might have remembered eight new words out of a list of 10, you may remember only two or three out of a list of 30.

Interference of one memory with another may act forwards or backwards in time. Information already stored in the long-term memory may interfere with the registration of new information in certain cases. (Psychologists refer to it as 'proactive inhibition', if you are a glutton for jargon terms).

Suppose you first attend a play-reading group where everyone is unknown to you, and you make strenuous efforts to learn everyone's name – you then go to a discussion group at which there is a totally different crowd of people and you make an equal effort to learn everyone's name. When you next attend the play-reading group you may find that the second lot of names has quite driven the first lot out of your head! (This is called 'retroactive inhibition' – inhibition in a backwards direction.)

How to avoid the effects of forwards and backwards inhibition and thus greatly increase your capacity for learning and remembering will be addressed later on in the book.

Repression. Chapters 2 and 4 deal with repression at some length, but here I would merely point out that it refers to motivated forgetting – the idea that you do not remember incidents that would not only cause anxiety but would arouse conflicts that you know you cannot resolve. The idea was popularized by Freud, but it is a very old one and is summed up in ancient sayings such as, 'There's none so blind as they that won't see'. The repressed memories are supposed to persist in the unconscious part of the mind and to continue to affect your actions in an irrational way.

Cue-dependent forgetting. Some information that you may think you have completely forgotten, and over which you have racked your brains in vain, may be retrieved by your coming across the appropriate cue. Thus a friend describes in detail a mutual acquaintance of long ago and you say you have not the faintest recollection of ever having known such a person – then your friend says 'Brighton' and the memory comes flooding back – the acquaintance you both made unwillingly in Brighton who was always to be met in the pubs there and who frequently tried to borrow money. We might equally well refer to 'cue-dependent remembering' for this class of information as its retrieval is heavily dependent on special cues. If you have lived a long time, and hence have a memory-bank that is very fully stocked, it is natural that some memories will refer to earlier parts of your life that you don't often think about, and are therefore specially dependent on cues to retrieve them, as in the instance I have just described.

DIFFERENT SORTS OF MEMORY
Let us return now to those systems of memory described earlier and talk about the different sorts of memories that are stored in the long-term memory-bank.

 Semantic memory. This concerns knowledge of such matters as – the meaning of words, that cows eat grass, that Norway is next to Sweden, in other words the huge body of factual information that you carry round with you. You dont know how or when you learned all this information, you just accept it as part of your basic equipment.

Episodic memory. Literally memory for episodes. You remember the events that have made up your total career more or less as a continuous narrative, although some events stand out more clearly than others, and some episodes may be forgotten or remembered incorrectly.

Procedural memory. You remember how to tie your tie, ride a bicycle and perform other skilled sequences of movements, but you would find it difficult to explain in words how you do it.

Iconic memory, etc. This is memory for pictures and other visual material. You can easily remember this name, as icons are pictures. If I were to show you a series of photographs of people's faces, and then shuffle these with a series that you had never seen, when presented with the mixed lot of photographs you would be able, with a fair degree of accuracy, to sort out those you had seen from those you had not. If I asked you how you knew that you had not seen the new pictures, you would be at a loss to explain. You would probably say that they just seemed unfamiliar to you. How the brain does this is one of the major problems of psychology. It is as though when you see an object, or a scene, you photograph it, and form a template of it, so that when you are looking at photographs, as described above, you compare them with the templates, and if they do not fit you are immediately conscious of the discrepancy. It is significant that it is easier to form more accurate templates of faces of people in one's own ethnic group. As one Chinese witness is alleged to have said when confronted with ten men at a police identity parade, 'No can do – all Westerners look alike.'

We might well add auditory memory – memory for the sounds you have heard – memory for smells and tastes, and memory for sensations. You can certainly remember tunes you have heard, and conjure them up in imagery. Similarly you can remember, and re-create in imagination to some degree, the impressions you have formed in the other senses. We humans are not so good at imagining tastes and smells, and that is why the food in dreams is said to be so tasteless, but I am sure that the dreams of dogs are a riot of exciting smells.

VISUAL MEMORY COMPARED WITH VERBAL MEMORY

The difference between the parts of the brain that deal with visual material and that which processes verbal material has been greatly exaggerated by some writers. It is not important for you to study the question of the localization of function in the brain, providing you get the idea that visual memories and verbal memories are processed rather differently, but you can remember things best if you employ all kinds of memory to anchor them in your memory-bank. If you think of a concrete object like a 'loaf', you can form a visual image of what is, for you, a typical loaf. You also have it anchored verbally by the sound of it, which is rather like 'love' and you also remember that 'to loaf' means to hang around lazily. You may also, because of the familiarity of sound, and the meaning of 'to loaf', fleetingly form a sentence, 'The oaf loafs around.' Thus words can be fixed in your memory-bank by both visual and verbal means. When we come to studying ways of remembering new material you will see how important it is to anchor such material by both visual and verbal means. Because you live in a literate culture you also have the advantage that things can be represented in writing – thus 'loaf' conjures up the letters LOAF in your memory.

Abstract nouns like 'health', 'beauty', 'spite', etc, are less easy to be represented visually, and are less easy to remember. Sometimes in talking you are lost for a word, and it is almost always an abstract word. 'It was simply a matter of – er – er – what's the word – spite.' You are less likely temporarily to lose a concrete word that can be visualized.

Sound imagery has some part in making words memorable, and words like 'click', 'hiss', 'gallop', 'murmur' are supposed to imitate the sound of the action they describe. Poets make use of this effect in some of their poems, as in Tennyson's lines:

The moan of doves in immemorial elms,
And the murmuring of innumerable bees.

which are intended to imitate these summer sounds. This effect delights in the term 'onomatopoeia', and one can sometimes get away with a made-up word that sounds right in a foreign country when the real word is elusive, like saying, "Donnez moi – er some 'clink-clink' – s'il vous plait," when presenting one's drink at the bar, having forgotten the French for ice.

THE MEMORY AS A LIBRARY

This analogy is one of the most useful ways of explaining how you learn, how you remember, and how you sometimes forget.

If you have only 20 books on your book shelf it is likely that you can easily pick out any one of them when you require it, and lay hands on it quickly. But if you possess several hundred books it is less easy to identify any one of them, and the search may take a little time. In order to get over this difficulty librarians classify books before they shelve them, and within each category there are sub-categories, and the books are shelved alphabetically by the authors' names. But on what basis are the books classified? A book might be classified under 'memoirs', or 'travel', or 'countryside'. So in your memory for the names of people you have just met, the Smiths might appear under 'school friends', 'past work-mates', 'Sussex neighbours', or a host of other headings.

A problem that besets big libraries is that new books may come in and pile up more rapidly than the staff can classify and shelve them, and this is precisely the problem with taking in new information quicker than you can sort it and file tidily in your memory-bank. One theory is that during the periods of sleep in which you are dreaming the mind is busily occupied with sorting out the inform-ation recently acquired and tidily attaching it to the right places in the brain. Those parts of the newly acquired material that can't be easily fitted in are then edited out, as it were, and this is what you may experience as dreams. It is hardly necessary to discuss this theory here, but in noting it you can get the idea of a memory-bank that is constantly being added to, edited and modified.

The library analogy makes it clear why you may have problems in remembering in later life, because the longer you live the greater amount of information there is to store away. These problems need have nothing to do with any supposed deterioration of the brain. How great your problems are depends upon the care you take in classifying the incoming material and storing it in orderly 'pigeon-holes' so that it can be easily retrieved. It also depends upon the suitability of the incoming material to be attached to what is already in the memory-bank, as the following account will demonstrate.

Someone I know, who was in her mid-60s, decided that she would like to take an Open University course in science, because she was totally ignorant of scientific matters, and felt rather at a loss with friends of a different educational background and experience. She worked very hard at her studies and passed the examination. To her dismay, however, she found that in a month or two she had entirely forgotten practically everything she had learned in the science course, and that she had to admit that it was largely a waste of her time.

Had she studied chemistry, physics and biology at school, even at quite an elementary level, then she would have had the basic structure of science, there in her memory-bank, and even though she might have 'forgotten' 90 per cent of the facts and formulae by her 60s, she would have had something relevant to build upon with the more advanced science of the Open University degree course. A more sensible course of action would have been to study the sort of science they teach children in the primary school, and having mastered that (which might have disabused her of some of the assumptions about the material world that many unscientific adults have) gone on to work toward 'O' level science, then to 'A' level, and finally to attempt degree studies. It is never too late in life to learn, and some adults find that the major difficulties that they have are concerned with un-learning the many fallacies that they have believed in all their lives.

THE MEMORY AS AN OFFICE

This is an analogy of the process of storing information and retrieving it which is alternative to the library analogy, which rather appeals to me, as in my untidy office I have problems of storage and retrieval rather similar to those I have with my memory. In my office I have an in-tray, an out-tray, and a filing cabinet in which all sorts of material is stored. I also have a shelf of great big box files in which a variety of material is stored, including, at the time of writing, the partly-written chapters of this book. When material is received in the post, it first goes into the in-tray, and then when I have had time to classify it, much of it either goes into the out-tray or directly into the filing cabinet or into one of the box files. Some of it, after I have glanced at it, goes into the wastepaper basket.

The in-tray corresponds to the short-term memory, and the filing cabinet and the box files to the long-term memory. The material that I throw directly into the wastepaper basket corresponds to most of that which enters my short-term memory and is of no permanent importance, so it never goes into my long-term memory-bank. It is lost for ever.

If I am being properly conscientious I deal with the more valuable material in my in-tray and then file it the appropriate file either in the cabinet or on the shelf. This is generally easy if it obviously belongs to a topic for which I already have a file (say, income tax) but in some cases I am a little uncertain as to where it properly belongs: should it be filed with general correspondence with publishers, or should it go with a file on a book I am planning that these publishers might accept ? Sometimes I am lazy and careless and just shove it in a file that is only remotely relevant. Occasionally it is quite unusual material for which I have no file, and I have to make a new one with a new label for it.

Now comes the problem of retrieval. Someone writes to me and asks me a question about the training of nurses and I go straight to the appropriate file and am I am able to tell them what I have recorded about this topic. Sometimes it is not so easy, as the relevant material might be filed in one of several files. This takes a little time, just as it would take you a little time to remember what you were doing in June 10 years ago. There are occasions on which I simply cannot answer the question at all as I can't retrieve the material as I carelessly mis-filed it, or made a new file for it but took no note of where I put the new file. Just occasionally I may have paid so little attention to a document when I received it that I threw it in the wastepaper basket although I think later on that I filed it, and this may happen with things you thought you learned but you never really worked on so they never went into your memory-bank.

I have a really huge amount of material stored in my office because I have worked there for many years, and I sometimes promise myself that I will go through the filing cabinet and reorganize it so that it will be easier to retrieve material, and I dare say that you have a huge amount stored in your memory-bank. If some of it is not easily accessible to you, you may think that you have 'forgotten' it. You may be under the impression that you have a 'bad memory' and blame your age, when all that is wrong is that in later life you know too much. If you once studied contract bridge, or Roman history, or bookkeeping, you may now imagine that you have 'forgotten it all for good'. But that knowledge could be retrieved (provided that you really wanted to remember it), if you unearthed the relevant file and reorganized it. The process of re-organization would, of course, mean that you made connections between some elements of this old material and the new knowledge that you have acquired in your later years. You might even find that you could now play bridge more effectively than you could long ago in your callow youth.

You should not stretch analogies too far, but if you ponder on the library analogy, and the organization of an office, you will begin to understand your memory and how to use it, with greater clarity.

2

NINE MYTHS ABOUT MEMORY

It is widely believed that our memory will inevitably decline and that there is little that we can do about it. Those doctors who take the patronizingly 'poor old thing' attitude towards their older patients, are reinforcing this belief. If you accept this myth, it may become a self-fulfilling prophesy: you don't expect to remember things properly, so cease to have any confidence in your own ability to learn. Organizations such as the University of the Third Age (U3A) and the Open University have demonstrated the falsity of this belief, but all too many people, in referring to themselves, think, 'Ah, that's all right for the very clever ones, but not for a poor old person like me!'

While I am concerned here primarily with the myths about memory in later life, the whole subject of false beliefs about memory must be examined, for only by gaining a realistic understanding of the nature of memory can we tackle the problems of different kinds of forgetfulness and learning.

1. IS YOUR BRAIN LESS EFFICIENT BECAUSE IT HAS SHRUNK?

It is true that the brain grows lighter during the course of our life. The average weight of the brain of a young adult male is about 1.41 kgm, and that of a young adult female 1.26 kgm. The smaller female brain does not imply that women have less mental ability – it merely reflects the fact that women are, on the whole, smaller than men, and brain weight is related to the total size of the body. The brain is made up of millions of brain cells (neurones), far more than you will ever need for your mental processes. These nerve cells take part in our thinking and storing of information only when they have become inter-connected in a vast neural network – surplus cells are constantly being shed throughout our lives, so that the brain of someone in their 90s will be significantly lighter than it was in their 20s. But this shrinkage has nothing whatever to do with loss of intellectual ability, for what is lost is surplus material, and the old / young difference may be compared with the man/woman difference in brain weight. It is tempting, of course, for the young to think of the brains of their grandparents as being like shrivelled walnuts within their shells!

2. WILL YOUR MENTAL CAPACITY WEAR OUT ?

Machines wear out with use, so if you think of a brain as a machine, it is not unnatural to assume it 'wears out' with age, and believe that people become stupid, forgetful, and generally less mentally efficient as they age. It is true that the arteries in the brain become less elastic with age, just as the skin becomes less elastic, so there is a growing danger of arteries rupturing if blood pressure is high. This sort of accident is known as a 'stroke'. But the neural tissue does not harden, and there is no 'wearing out' of the brain.

We really don't know much about the details of how messages are conveyed along the nerves, and passed from one nerve cell to another at a 'synapse', but it has been suggested that with ageing the messages are conveyed more slowly – this is a speculation for which there is little firm evidence.

If there have been a number of ruptures of arteries over a period of time then there will be actual destruction of brain tissue and there may be a dramatic decline in mental ability which is known as 'multi-infarct dementia'. This can happen at an early age with boxers who have been hit about the head too often and too seriously, and they are referred to as being 'punch drunk'.

Ideas about the deterioration of the brain with age are all mixed up with fears about brain diseases such as Alzheimer's disease. But diseases are diseases, and are not to be confused with the ageing of healthy tissue. We shall deal with brain diseases in a separate chapter.

3. CAN YOU USE UP MENTAL CAPACITY ?

There is a naive idea that one has a certain amount of 'mental capacity' which can be used up and leave one, as it were, mentally bankrupt. The same idea has been applied to sexual capacity by some people– they imagined that if one is fully sexually active in middle life then one will be drained of all passion in the later years. This latter myth was seriously propagated by medical doctors in the 19th century, and went by the name of 'entropy', a term borrowed from physics. In actual fact the exact opposite is true both for mental and sexual capacity – the more active you are in youth and middle life, the more active you are likely to be in the years after retirement. By being intellectually active we build up a richly equipped mind and we can go on adding to its richness all the days of our lives. The great musician Pablo Casals continued to practise his cello in his 90s every day, and it is reported that when a student asked him why he did so he replied, 'Because I continue to improve.'

4. CAN MEMORY BE IMPROVED
BY 'EXERCISES' SIMILAR TO PHYSICAL WORK-OUTS ?

The efficiency of memory can be improved by various techniques that depend upon understanding more about ourselves and how memory functions, but memory should not be compared with muscular strength that can be enhanced by physical exercises. I have by me a page from a popular newspaper that sets out exercises to be performed daily with the object of improving one's 'mental powers'. The author writes:

The format is familiar to anyone who has done any kind of physical exercise -- warming up, strengthening and finally cooling down ...
You already know the advantages of warming up your body – the same principles apply to warming up your mind. It will allow you to per-
form more effectively when it really counts. These exercises are meant to help you with mental functions like list-making, memory, word visualisation and comprehension.

There follows a series of exercises such as counting down from 100 to one as quickly as possible, reciting 20 names as quickly as possible, numbering them as you go, naming 20 types of food as quickly as possible and numbering them, and similar pointless exercises. The person who devised this does not give any rationale for why this should be beneficial, nor any indication that she has tested, by proper research methods, whether the exercises have any effect whatsoever. It is significant that the whole idea started with a tennis champion, who naturally exercised his muscles and his tennis skill frequently, trying to improve his mental ability by naively trying to do the equivalent with his brain! He said: 'I remember feeling as if I were working mental muscles I'd never worked before.' Unfortunately mental processes do not operate in any way comparable to muscular action.

5. IS 'REPRESSION' A MYTH ?

The idea of 'repression' is very ancient but Freud popularized the concept and made it central to his psychoanalytic theory. Stated very simply, it is proposed that you remember a very great deal more than you can become aware of, and many incidents are stored away in the 'unconscious' part of the mind and prevented from rising to consciousness because recognition of them would cause us intolerable anxiety. At the level of common sense there is certainly a germ of truth in this since it is unpleasant to think about all the horrid, embarrassing and distasteful things that have happened to you at one time or another, and so you can refer to such memories as being 'repressed'. However, you also know from your experience that there may be unpleasant incidents that you remember all too often, although you would like to blot out such incidents from your recall. If there is some kind of 'censor' keeping some memories out of consciousness, as Freud suggested, it is a very inefficient censor!

Repression may also refer to the language you use. I remember that my sister, first studying medicine as a young student, was quite shocked to hear the dreadfully coarse language that some respectable old ladies used when they became half-conscious as they went under the ether anaesthesia that was then in use. They would never have used such awful words in their normal waking life, but ether had the effect of disinhibiting them, and 'repressed' language was released.

The question of repression has been, and still is, a subject of contention among psychologists. There was a great vogue for attempting to test Freudian ideas in psychological laboratories in the 1930s, particularly the concept of repression. Do you, in fact, carry around with you a whole set of memories of which you are unconscious because they were generated in particularly stressful circumstances? It is not ethically permissible, of course, to subject people to greatly stressful experiences in the laboratory (although some experimental psychologists went pretty far!) but it was argued that if certain tasks were associated with rather unpleasant and embarrassing circumstances, and others were not, repression would tend to make the former type of task less well remembered than the latter.

Of course one cannot reproduce in the laboratory the psychological conditions that exist in the real world, so the results of these experiments were indecisive.

If you want to try a more real-life experiment for yourself, do the following before you read on. Simply write down, in your own time, say, 10 or more events that you remember very well happening to you in the first eight years of your life. It may take you a little while to do this, but if you concentrate you will probably remember at least 10.

When you have finished your list, mark against each of the events P (if it was pleasant), or U (unpleasant) or N (neutral). Psychologists who have tried this experiment have found that with most people the proportions tend to be thus: P = 50%, U = 30%, N = 20%.

Could it be that people repress the more unpleasant memories of childhood so they are really unavailable to them, or is it that they merely prefer to think about the more pleasant events, although they

could perfectly well recall all the unpleasant ones if they wished to ?
If you are of an inquiring mind and wish to do this little experiment
with your friends, do not tell them in advance that you will ask them
to put the P, U and N ratings on their list when it is complete. And
– most important – in order that they will be quite frank, assure
them in advance that you don't want to see their list and they should
keep it entirely secret!

There may be an explanation alternative to that of repression. The
study of people who have witnessed or been victims of crimes or accidents has been undertaken by those who are experts in 'eyewitness
testimony'. It is obviously important that witnesses should be able to
recall the happenings correctly. The question arises whether witness-
ing, or experiencing as a victim, a particularly traumatic event such
as a violent robbery, causes repression because of its unpleasantness,
or does it make the event particularly memorable ?

   A survey of 235 American lawyers revealed that 82% of defence
lawyers believed that a high level of emotion at the time would make
it difficult for people to remember accurately the faces of those
involved in the incident, but only 32% of lawyers concerned with
prosecution were of this opinion. Experiments with volunteers have
yielded no very clear-cut answers. People have been shown a film in
which a staged event of extreme violence occurs, and then had their
memory for the various events tested. Results generally show that
the violent event is indeed emotionally arousing in the viewers, and
that it is recalled better than the neutral events, but that memory for
all the details of it is rather poor. This is what tends to happen in
real life: a witness may very well remember that she saw a man

being assaulted and stabbed, but she may have surprisingly little memory for the appearance of the attacker. All she can remember is the shocking sight of the knife and the blood, but the peripheral details of the incident seem to be blotted out. It seems hardly reasonable to attribute the lack of memory to the mechanism of 'repression', for the gory details that shocked her are remembered very well. What you remember depends on what you perceive at the time, and emotional shock tends to concentrate your attention on just one salient aspect of an incident to the exclusion of all that you would have noted and remembered in a calmer state of mind.

6. DID ALL THAT YOU REMEMBER OCCUR THE WAY YOU THINK IT DID ?

Repression and false memory have been in the news lately. Some psychotherapists, strongly influenced by the extreme wing of the feminist movement, have advanced an extraordinary theory – that practically all neurotic trouble in adult women has been caused by sexual abuse in early childhood about which they remember nothing because all memory of it has been 'repressed'. In the 1890s Freud did indeed suspect that this might have been the case with some of his neurotic patients, but he eventually came to think that such 'memories' were due to sexual fantasies rather than any events that had really taken place.

The modern psychotherapists who are promoting this idea, in a long course of therapy, persuade women patients that they have suffered horrid abuse from their fathers or other male figures, and the fact that they have no memory for any such mistreatment is due to the mechanisms of 'repression'. There is a great deal of evidence, going back over a century, that it is perfectly possible, with or without hypnosis, to create false memories in people, particularly when they are in a condition of emotional dependence on a therapist. These psychotherapists go further: not only do they get their patients to believe that they have been sexually abused in childhood, even when they come from the most normal families, but they persuade them

that it is necessary for them to hate the male figures they have iden-
tified as the abusers, and to take revengeful action against them.
This has led to a number of court cases in the USA, women suing
their fathers for damages, and, of course, the break-up of previously
harmonious family relationships.*

---

* The practice of this extraordinary variety of psychotherapy began in North
America, and it has now spread to Britain, so that the The British False Memory
Society has been formed to 'sponsor, conduct and publish research into the phenomenon of False Memory'. Among its activities it offers support to families
affected by the phenomenon of False Memory, and offers advice on access to legal
assistance. It is sponsored by many people eminent in the academic, legal and
clinical world.

7. CAN HYPNOSIS RECOVER ALL MEMORIES ACCURATELY?

Hypnosis is associated with many folk-myths, some of them quite
absurd, but believed in by many people. It has been remarked that
hypnotism exists in some form in all cultures and the practice of it
has grown out of magic. In Western Europe we can trace its growth
since the 18th century when the practice of mesmerism began, taking
its name from Anton Mesmer, a Viennese doctor who practised in
Paris. Although hypnotism as we know it today is not quite the same
thing as mesmerism, it has inherited many of the myths that the
mesmerists promoted, one of them being that it was possible for
hypnotized subjects to remember accurately everything that had ever
occurred – even their own birth.

The question of the supposed recovery of accurate memory by
means of hypnosis highlights the inaccurate concept of memory that
is very commonly held. For more than a century we have become
accustomed to accepting the fact that past events can be stored on
films, gramophone records and magnetized tapes. Therefore it is not
unnatural to think of memory being stored in the brain in some comparable manner, and that we have simply to activate that part of the
brain to get an accurate recall of what is stored there.

This incorrect concept of memory was reinforced by some experiments that were done by Dr Penfield over 30 years ago. He was operating on the brains of patients who suffered from epilepsy in order to remove injured tissue that produced fits, an operation that is performed under local anaesthesia with the patient conscious, because brain tissue feels no pain. He found that when he stimulated certain points some patients would report experiencing 'memories' of events of long ago. Thus it certainly seemed that it was at these points that memories were stored – as on a videotape. However, this phenomenon occurred only with a tiny proportion of the many patients on whom he operated. Indeed there was no proof that real memories were being activated – it might have been that the patients were having fantasies during the operation. It was also found that when these spots were surgically removed, it did not destroy the memory that appeared to be associated with them, so it is evident that other areas of the brain were also associated with the memories.

When you recall an event quite vividly, seeing, hearing and touching are frequently involved all together in the memory, and impressions conveyed by these three senses are received, and presumably stored, in different parts of the brain. It seems best therefore, to conceive of the act of recall as an act of reconstruction, a blending together of impressions from different parts of the brain. The idea that memory is to some extent a creative process is confirmed by all sorts of phenomena that I shall be discussing later in this book.

To return to the question of the enhancement of memory by hypnosis, the myths about it have never quite died out. During the 1970s there was a great vogue of trying to improve the memory of witnesses in police investigations in the USA. A school for police officers was set up in which they were taught that everything a person has ever seen, heard, and felt, is accurately stored in the brain as on a videotape, and by means of hypnosis any part of the mental videotape could be closely examined. They were told that not only could the hypnotized witnesses run this mental videotape backwards and forwards, but they could 'zoom in' on any detail in order to inspect it! That this was utter fantasy was pointed out by many knowledgeable psychologists who were appalled that such nonsense was being taught, yet nevertheless this era of teaching policemen to hypnotize, and convincing them of the super-normal powers of hypnosis, had its heyday in the 1970s. Many miscarriages of justice were attributable to it, and responsible jurists became deeply concerned . Finally state after state forbade policemen to use hypnosis, and even when the hypnosis was carried out by qualified psychologists, it was held that witnesses who had been hypnotized should not give evidence in court, because their testimony might be contaminated by false memories generated in the hypnotic session.

To give a typical example of what might happen in hypnosis, consider the following. A man witnessed a robbery taking place, and the thieves driving away in a car, but he could not remember the licence number on the rear of the car. The police had him hypnotized, and the hypnotist pressed and pressed him to re-live the event and to read out the rear number-plate as though it were actually there in front of him. Eventually he produced a number. The delighted police traced the number of the car, only to find that it belonged to a local headmaster, and when they approached him he had proof that his car had been in its garage at the time of the robbery. This sort of error, the creating of a false memory, is typical of what may happen with hypnosis. The witness had obviously seen the local headmaster's car on a number of occasions but taken no special note of its number plate. When he was in hypnosis, however, and desperately searching for a licence number, he innocently grafted, as it were, his memory of the headmaster's car on to his memory for the robbers getaway car. Had the number he produced not belonged to the car of a respectable local citizen who had proof of its whereabouts at the critical time, some poor innocent motorist might have been arrested and charged with involvement in the robbery.

I was involved with a somewhat similar case quite recently in my capacity as an expert witness to the courts. In 1988 the notorious 'motorway murder case' occurred: an unfortunate woman whose car had broken down on the M50 motorway was abducted by a passing motorist while telephoning for help, and some days later her murdered body was discovered close to the motorway. It so happened that another motorist had observed a car drawing up beside this woman, and he assumed that its driver was giving her help. When this key witness (who happened to be a police inspector off duty) heard that the woman was missing and presumably had been abducted, he informed his police colleagues and the hunt began for the suspected car.

Unfortunately, the witness could not recall the licence number of the car, and the senior police officer in charge of the case, naively believing in the mythology of hypnosis, had him hypnotized to improve his memory. This action was strictly irregular, for he neglected to follow the very definite Guidelines that had been issued by the Home Office about the use of hypnosis in police investigations. In the hypnosis session, which was recorded on videotape, the hypnotist tried very hard to get the witness to re-live the experience of being behind the suspected car.

The witness first made some statements about what the number plate was not (except that he said it was definitely a C registration), and eventually he produced an actual number after a lot of coaxing by the hypnotist. He also made some statements about the appearance of the car. When the police tried to trace the licence number that he purported to remember, they found that it was a registration that did not exist – it was the product of the witness' hypnotic fantasy. Police inquiries on other lines led to the arrest of a man who was charged with the murder, found guilty, and sentenced to life imprisonment.

The police did not reveal to the Defence that the key witness had been hypnotized, and that during the hypnosis session he had made statements that would virtually have exonerated the car the accused was driving, both with regard to the registration number and some details of its appearance, if taken seriously. This was most irregular, but it became known to the prisoner's Defence only by chance some years later, and formed the main basis for an appeal against conviction to the High Court. The appeal was allowed and the sentence was quashed. My own opinion was that the witness should never have been hypnotized – he was a perfectly competent man and the hypnosis session only served to confuse him. That it did not serve to reveal the real registration number of the car he saw is quite certain because he produced a registration that did not exist.

The idea that hypnosis can really re-instate memories that you have forgotten is not entirely a myth but the matter is rather complex. In the 1950s there were some experiments that appeared to show that hypnosis had indeed a remarkable power to re-instate long-forgotten memories. For instance, it is possible with a highly responsive subject to get him or her to go back to childhood in imagination and behave like a child of the suggested age. In this condition the hypnotized subject can be asked about events that are contemporary with the suggested age, and in this condition adult subjects will prattle away about their childhood life and give quite a wealth of detail about their school and school-mates. When asked to do a drawing they will execute it in a very childlike manner, and their writing will be very immature.

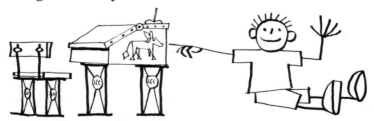

What the early experimenters failed to do was to check on the accuracy of the details recalled: did Miss Smith at the age of six really have a schoolmate called Bunty with long blonde pigtails? Did Mr Jones at the same age really sit in the corner of a schoolroom at a desk that had a picture of a donkey scratched on it? Often it is very difficult to check on the accuracy of such graphic details – they may simply be the product of fantasy. When the drawings of hypnotized subjects regressed to childhood were shown to an expert in children's drawings he said that they were not typical of children and indicated 'sophisticated over-simplification'. It seemed that the adults regressed to childhood were really play-acting and putting on a performance of behaviour that they believed would have typified the age in question. Perhaps some of their memories were real and genuine, but later evidence implied that they were mixed with fantasy.

Other experiments compared the behaviour of genuinely hypnotized subjects regressed to childhood, adult actors pretending to be children at the specified ages, and actual children at these ages. The hypnotically regressed subjects behaved much more like the actors than the real children. It was also found that the childhood memories of the hypnotized subjects were no better than that of the actors, as far as verifiable details went. These more sophisticated experiments indicated that although hypnotic age-regression may encourage people to talk a lot about their childhood, the real memories recalled are all mixed up with fantasy and guessing.

In yet another experiment a group of students were required to learn Longfellow's *Village Blacksmith*, and a year later, without prior warning, were tested on it. One half of the group were tested in their normal waking state, and one half were tested while hypnotized, with strong suggestions that their memory would be greatly improved. To the delight of the experimenters it was found that the hypnotized students wrote much more and appeared to have a superior recall of the poem. However, careful analysis showed that although more was written by those hypnotized, as far as accurate recall went, the groups were just about equal. What hypnosis does is to increase people's confidence in their memory, and they are far more willing to guess and 'chance their arm'. Thus some who wrote a lot were merely padding their productions with verses they composed after the manner of Longfellow! This rather long discussion of hypnosis with regard to memory has been necessary to make clear that memory at any age is not a hard and fast record that can be consulted as you consult a diary, a dictionary or a videotape. The process of retrieval from memory is a creative process, and it is easy to be too creative in our normal, waking life, grafting one memory on to another, and mistaking fantasized events for real events.

8. DOES THE 'ABSENT-MINDED OLD PROFESSOR' REALLY EXIST ?

I am not sure that I should refer to this as a 'myth' as there is a lot of truth in certain aspects of it, but the matter is complex and raises some paradoxical issues concerning ageing. First you should note that this stock character is not necessarily absent-minded because of his age, but because of the burden of many competing responsibilities and intellectual problems he has to bear in his professorial job. Young people who have not yet climbed up the promotional ladder, do not have to bear so many responsibilities, and so they are less conspicuously absent-minded. This character typifies a deficiency in what is known as 'prospective memory', that is, forgetting to do things that are planned for the future: he forgets appointments – he forgets that friends have been asked for supper – he fails to collect the books from the library on his way home. With an over-crowded and sometimes ill-classified memory-bank, our 'Professor' is less likely to give the right response when the appropriate cue arrives (11 o'clock – now go and see the Librarian).

9. CAN YOU TEACH AN OLD DOG NEW TRICKS ?

Whether you can teach new tricks to an old dog depends principally on whether he really wants to learn them. The surest way of becoming a very old dog is to stop learning new tricks – that much is certain – and indeed, you may become a dead dog before you expect it. For as one eminent and experienced psychologist observed, 'When the mind ceases to deal with novelty the body begins to die'.

Although the principal reason for older people not learning new things is that they simply don't want to, the lack of motivation is often due to the general idea that you cannot remember things properly in later life, and this belief saps people's self-confidence. Memory difficulties occur at all ages and they are blamed on different things. In your 20s you may have blamed a series of sad love affairs ('That's why I failed so many exams!'). In your 30s you may have blamed a wretchedly bad memory on difficulties at work ('With all this hassle how can I be expected to remember my mother's birth-day?'). In your 40s there may have been family troubles to blame, and, in your 50s – but need I go on? Suffice it to say that in your 60s and onwards there will always be your age to blame, and one of the things you do forget is how bad you were at remembering things when you were younger!

The popularity with older people of the courses run by the Open University, the University of the Third Age (U3A), and other such organisations, shows that you can certainly learn new things if you really want to at any age, providing you are not unwell. For most people, skills that depend heavily on visual and spatial abilities begin to decline from the 20s onward, but verbal skills may increase in later life if you are actively engaged in working at things that involve verbal ability. If indeed an old dog says 'To hell with that – now I'm retired I can get along very nicely without learning new tricks', that is a personal choice – but the old dog should realize what is in store for him.

3

HOW IS YOUR MEMORY CHANGING ?

You are getting older and you have probably noticed that your memory is changing in various ways. You probably regard it as 'getting worse', because that's the conventional idea, but it is a complex matter to say exactly what 'worse' means. It is more useful to consider what changes, if any, you have noticed taking place.

Let us consider one change that tends to occur as you age – a difficulty in remembering names. You are introduced to new people and very soon after you simply cannot remember their names. You ask a friend 'Who is the fellow with the beard?' His name is spoken again, yet soon after it has slipped out of your mind. The trouble with names is that, as Humpty Dumpty pointed out, generally they don't mean anything. If a name is unusual it is more likely to be remembered: 'This is Ambrose Smellie' – almost automatically you sniff and then think of ambrosia. You are likely to remember his name. But if his name is John Smith how are you to remember that ? You have known dozens of Johns and umpteen Smiths in your time; how are you to pigeon-hole this one in your memory-bank? This instance gives a useful clue as to what is happening as you get older; the memory-bank is perfectly sound, but it is getting over-stocked.

The storing of books in a library is a useful analogy. As pointed out in Chapter 1, the same book might be classified under 'memoirs', or 'travel', or 'countryside'. So in your memory the Smiths might appear under 'school friends', 'past work-mates', 'Sussex neighbours', or a host of other headings. And where are you going to file away this new Smith you have just met – among 'arty party-goers'?

WHAT TO DO ABOUT MEETING NEW PEOPLE
First of all, note that forgetting is not always 'failing' to remember;

forgetting can have a necessary and positive function, wiping the mind clear of unnecessary information. Why do you forget some people's names ? Often because there is no earthly reason why you should bother to remember them. Everybody realizes this is so, and if it is obvious that someone has forgotten your name, it implies that you are of no importance to them, and you may feel a little hurt. The first thing you must do if you really want to remember the name of someone you are introduced to is to work on it immediately. Remember, you transfer new impressions from the short-term memory to the long-term store only by working on them.

You must make it mean something to you. It doesn't matter how absurd the associations are that you make to the new name, and often the absurder and more humorous the association the better. You don't have to tell Ambrose Smellie what you are thinking when you shake his hand! It is best to consider what to do on meeting new people in terms of four steps:

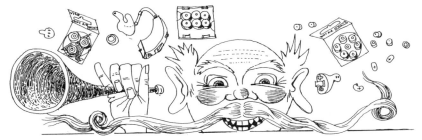

1. Make sure that you get the name right. One common reason for the name not being remembered is that it was never heard properly in the first place. This sounds such common sense that you may think it is not worth mentioning it. Reduced sharpness of hearing is very common in later life, and for some reason people are ashamed of their partial deafness and try to hide it. Many people who should wear hearing aids to make life more comfortable refuse to do so because, for them, it is the badge of a pathetic oldie.

Funnily enough, about 50 years ago many people (especially women) were ashamed to wear spectacles, and went around half-

blind, cutting their friends in the street. You may have heard
Dorothy Parker's couplet:

Men don't make passes
At girls who wear glasses.

But nowadays well-designed and attractive glasses are common, and
nobody minds saying, 'Wait till I put my glasses on then I'll look at
it.' But people are generally too embarrassed to say, 'Wait till I put
my hearing aid in and then you can tell me about it.'

So if you want to remember the name of the person to whom you
are being introduced you must make sure that you have heard the
name correctly. Never be too shy to say, 'I'm sorry; did you say
Foster or Forrester?' The mere fact of your saying the name, and
getting it repeated, will probably fix it in your memory very well.
Never seem to blame you own hearing; imply that the other person is
mumbling and should really learn to speak up!

An apparent change in your power of learning and retaining
names in later life may have nothing to do with memory – it may be
wholly attributable to gradual fading of the acuity of your hearing. If
something has not been assimilated, of course it cannot be retrieved
from the memory-bank. You may need to get a hearing aid; you don't
think it odd that you needed to begin wearing spectacles in your 40s
or earlier, so why not accept that your hearing may need a boost later
on?

**2. Take a careful look at the person's face and general
appearance.** First impressions are often highly misleading; someone
may at first strike you as being cunning and sophisticated, and it
soon turns out that he is a simple and trusting soul – but that does
not matter. If his face appears to you 'foxy' because of the narrow
eyes and lean jaws, by all means think of him thus in memorizing his
name. If you are lucky his name may fit with this impression and
you privately call him 'Foxy Ferguson' (an alliterative help), but if his
name happens to be Clark, you may just make do with 'Foxy Clark'.
But don't tie yourself to one method of remembering names; be

flexible and use several. His name is Clark so see him as a cunning solicitor's clerk.

The impression that faces make on people has been the subject of a great deal of research, and many people (including Leonardo da Vinci) have proposed quite unsound methods of remembering faces by analysing them. It is you who is going to remember the face, and so let your own personal fantasy rip. If someone looks quite angelic to you, treasure that first impression in finding a memorable tag to his name. If his name is Bulstrode dub him 'Beatific Bulstrode', if it is Chalmers, call him 'The Charming Chalmers' – if it is Dixon, dub him 'Dick's Angelic Son', and think how unlike your friend Dick he looks. (I could go through the alphabet like this.) It does not matter in the least that you soon find him to be the reverse of angelic when you have talked to him a little – his name then becomes memorable because it is ironical.

I advise concentrating on the face first, while the name is buzzing around in your short-term memory. Don't be in a hurry; delay a bit while you take in the face and general appearance. Once you have formed a template of the face in your visual memory, then you can get busy fitting the name to it. It is useless to remember names, and then have difficulty in fitting them to the right faces, but you have this marvellous and mysterious capacity of making templates of human faces (especially of your own ethnic group) so make use of it and really look at people when you are introduced and not at their toe-caps.

3. What does the name mean? As Humpty Dumpty said, 'What does Alice mean?' People complain that the trouble with names is that they do not mean anything, so how can they be retained? But many names do mean something, and if they do not, they can be made to. Mr Aldred, Mrs Baker, Mrs Carver, Mr Dane, Miss Easton – I have just run my eye down a huge list of names and there are very few which do not immediately suggest something. The names of trades and occupations are easy, but most names can be made to mean something, as with Aldred = All Dread (he must be a very unpopular person), and Easton = East Town. Immediately you have fixed on the meaning of the name, connect it with the impression the man or woman has made on you. In your private thoughts you may not always be very polite about people, but do not discard impressions and names because they are derogatory. They are private to you. There are jokes about people coming out with private nicknames unintentionally, and greeting Mrs Bumstead with 'Hallo, Mrs Bum', but I have never known it happen in real life.

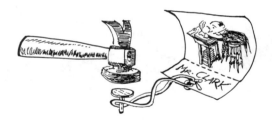

4. Use the name. You will not fix the name firmly in your memory-bank unless you use it. Once you have formed your impression of the face and appearance of the person, and linked it to your version of the name, you must try to use the name as soon as possible. If you address him, preface the remark with his name: 'Mr Clark, I wonder if you . . .' Or if you have no immediate opportunity of addressing him personally, when speaking to someone else, you can say something like, 'I've just met Mr Clark, and he . . .' If it is important to remember the name then write it down as soon as you can, and record the impression: 'Foxy Clark'. People who forget the names of those they are introduced to tend to be shy – they do not look properly at their new acquaintances, and are too diffident to make up humorous, apt, fanciful, rude, and memorable associations to both face and name. If you are going to remember peoples names, you must try to conquer your shyness in this respect.

You should now realize that with your overstocked memory-bank, names will not automatically register if you just passively listen to them. When you were a child with a mind like a fairly blank screen, names would stick much more readily, but when you are older you have to work on them if you want to remember them. But even so, the rate and quantity of the incoming material is important at any age.

When I was 13 years of age I went to a boarding school and was confronted with the names of hundreds of boys, and for weeks I was calling boys by the wrong names and getting myself unpopular by doing so. For it may be much more hurtful to call someone by the wrong name than to admit that you don't remember his name at all, and this goes for adults of all ages too. You may be particularly unlucky if you call Thompson 'Jackson', and the latter happens to be a great slob whom Thompson heartily dislikes.

As already mentioned, it often does not matter if you remember some people's names or not, so why bother? If it is totally unimportant at a social gathering, you may go on thinking of other more interesting things as you shake other guests by the hand, and smile and look interested. But if, apart from special instances, it is important to remember everyone's name (say, you are going to be an official of a club) a very great deal can be done if you understand the nature of the problems you are faced with now you are older, if you are prepared to make the necessary effort. It is untrue and defeatist if you say to yourself 'How can an old person like me be expected to remember all these people's names? My brain is not what it used to be.' Your brain is perfectly all right; it is merely a question of it being a larger organization than it used to be, hence requiring more planning in its operation, like any other organization that develops in complexity.

By the nature of some people's occupation or special position it may be highly advantageous to them to take a lot of trouble over remembering individuals' names. It is reported that Napoleon remembered the names of all his officers in the various regiments, and some personal details about them, and this simple device of addressing them personally and showing that he knew who they were was very powerful in securing their loyalty and devotion. Important executives in industry and business can greatly increase their popularity and the morale of their staff by addressing them by their names. Such people get into the habit of learning names, and it is little trouble to them to do so once they have acquired the necessary techniques.

WHAT METHOD SUITS YOU BEST ?
Later in this book we shall discuss the question of individual differences, that is the way different people learn new information and store it. This is certainly relevant to how they devise their techniques for rapid and efficient learning. Some people are visualizers who make a great of use of mental pictures; others make use of the sound of words, and can memorize whole sentences very easily, including the local accent in which they were spoken. You must discover for yourself just what type of thinking and memorizing comes most easily to you, and this will become more apparent as you go through this book.

A PRACTICAL EXERCISE

It is often necessary not only to learn to associate names with people, but to learn what first names go with surnames. Mary Smith may feel hurt if you call her Mary Jones, for the latter may be notorious for her stupidity. One of the well-known pioneers of the study of memory, Hermann Ebbinghaus, wanted to study how we learn what goes with what by using what he called 'nonsense syllables'. These were short syllables that did not mean anything, like TEG MAS KEL that could be spoken but, being devoid of meaning, could be memorized without personal associations intruding – or so Ebbinghaus thought. He used himself as an experimental subject and learned long lists of associated nonsense syllables such as:

TEG – MAS

KAL – JOP

FIL – WES

With incredible patience, having learnt such lists he then used to study such things as how long it took for memory to decay, as when he found that he was connecting TEG with WES instead of with MAS. Students studying Psychology used to be given such boring exercises to do, but nowadays their studies are more connected with real-life problems. I give seminars for retired people and I usually start with everyone in the group of about 12 learning the names of every one of their class-mates. It is very useful as well as being instructive. If you would like to carry out a real-life exercise, try the following:

Spend about five minutes learning the following list of names, and then close the book and write down what you can remember of the list on a sheet of paper.

OLIVE FENWICK   FELICITY ORR

SARAH WINGS   MILES WHITE

OSWALD TIMMS   CHARLES FITCH

PETER FARR

Now open the book and check what you have written with the list on the page, Ask yourself the following questions and write down the answers:

1. How many first names did you get right ?

2. How many surnames did you get right ?

3. How many correct connections did you make ?

Don't be disappointed if your totals are small, for you are still learning about yourself and how you can operate most efficiently. Try to think how you set about the task. Was it the sound of the names that went together that made them stick ? Or did you form peculiar mental pictures of them, such as a Sarah you know equipped with angel's wings, Miles covered in white flour ? By trial and error in different learning situations you will learn what method suits you personally. Some people may prefer to treat it just as a list of words, and here is one method for learning such a list: note the initial letters of each name and you get O, F, S, W, O, T, P, F, F, O, M, W, C, F. Now using these initial letters, make up a sentence of 14 words that means something to you, such as 'Old Friends Stay With Other Times Perhaps For Friendship Or Merry White Christmas Fun.' The sentence may be utter nonsense, but as long as it sounds right to you that is all that matters. Having constructed your own sentence you have a key, a skeleton on which you can construct the original list of names.

When medical students are learning anatomy they often depend on such devices for learning long lists of names, and sometimes the sentences they construct are rather coarse. Medical student folklore contains anecdotes of students undergoing an examination, and when asked a question about some anatomical detail, coming out with some coarse word instead of the proper anatomical term it represents in a well-known jingle. But this is due to examination nerves! Now try out one or two of the methods suggested above, then close the book and try to write the list of names. I'll bet that you greatly improve on your first effort.

MISTAKING PHYSICAL FOR MENTAL CHANGES

The mistake of thinking that changes in your ability to hear were due to fading powers of memory is paralleled in a lot of other areas. You accept that you cannot run round the block as quickly as when you were younger – there is nothing odd about that. Perhaps you don't realize how many other physical changes are taking place with ageing. One change that most people do not know about refers to the dependence of the ability to learn on the level of the blood sugar that nourishes the brain.

Have you given up eating breakfast because you fear that you are putting on too much weight? Just consider this: a group of psychologists wanted to examine the relationship between blood-sugar level and the ability to learn, so they invited a group of young people, and older people, to come for an experiment in the morning. They were all asked to skip breakfast on that day. Both the young and the older group were then given a drink of a slightly sweet liquid; half the drinks were sweetened with saccharine, and half with glucose, a form of sugar that is not very sweet so you can take a lot of it without noticing. They were then given tests of learning and memory.

For the young group, it made no difference to their performance which drink they had been given, but the older people showed a better ability to remember if they had had glucose in their drink. That this was due to a difference in the level of their blood sugar was confirmed by testing samples of their blood. The level of sugar in our blood varies according to the time of day, when last we ate, etc., and, as we age this variation becomes greater, so if older people skip their breakfast they may find their memory faulty until after lunch, and a mid-morning snack may set things right.

The popular belief that the memory inevitably declines quite drastically with ageing has been reinforced by the earlier researches of psychologists which were faulty in many ways, and confused physical decline with mental decline. In more recent years psychologists have tried to rectify their earlier mistakes. An age-related change is in speed; just as older people are slower in running round the block, so they do psychological tests more slowly. Factors such as stiff finger joints, slightly impaired vision and hearing, all show up in testing with the psychologist's stopwatch. Because their movements are habitually slower, older people appear to be less bright than they are on psychological tests. In my dealings with young psychologists in training, I have noticed that the results obtained from their testing of older people sometimes reflected the dimness of the tester rather than that of the testee! Some would tend to mumble their questions and the testee was either too polite or too shy to say, 'Come on, speak up now, loud and clear! And how do you expect me to see your pictures properly in this poor light, even though it may be all right for your young eyes?'

The earlier researches of psychologists gave rise to all sorts of misapprehensions that are still affecting the self-image of older people and created the self-fulfilling prophesy about memory performance previously referred to. One of the important sources of error was that investigators would often base their findings on what is known as 'cross-sectional research'. They would test the abilities of groups of people in their 80s, 70s, 60s, 50s and compare the results with those from groups of people in their 20s, 30s and 40s. If you do it this way you get a huge apparent drop in ability with age. However, this method is fallacious because in each of the older age groups there are a number of individuals who are on their last legs and are about to fall off their perches, even in the 50s group, although their debility is not obvious. These people are by no means typical of their age, but they bring the group average down. In the younger age groups, although some individuals will soon die, they are not a significant minority There is a much greater variability in psychological test scores among older people than exists among younger people, because physical health affects both ability and motivation. While some people in their 90s are still hale and hearty, others in their 50s are beginning to suffer from the insidious effects of progressive conditions such as heart degeneration, cancer, and cerebrovascular disease that will eventually bring them to their graves.

One well-known test of intelligence, which is known as the WAIS, gives two IQ scores, a verbal and a performance IQ. It is a general finding that older people have a higher verbal IQ than their performance IQ, and this difference reflects the fact that while the items of the performance tests are timed with a stopwatch, the verbal tests are not. As pointed out above, as you age, you get less dextrous and quick in your movements, so the difference is due to physical factors rather than mental ones.

Another important source of error in researches up to about the 1960s was that the sort of older people who were tested were by no means typical of their age group because they lived in old people's homes, or attended clinics, and thus were readily available because they were partly dependent on the medical and social services. How atypical they were may be judged from the fact that only about 3% of pensioners live in old people's homes. Manifest intelligence and the ability to learn and remember are affected not only by physical health, but by mental health. It is not surprising that the tiny minority of pensioners who are forced to live in institutions because they cannot manage for themselves, and sometimes feel that nobody really wants them, have every reason to be depressed. Depression is a powerful cause of people, young or old, appearing to be stupid and having great difficulty in learning and remembering.

In the 1960s better methods of research began to be applied more widely, and longitudinal investigations began to show a different picture of the process of ageing. In longitudinal research you take the same individuals and study them over a period of many years, keeping a record of their physical health and manifest mental ability. Psychologists, medical researchers and other investigators then realized that a lot of what was supposed to be happening with ageing was fallacious. In the matter of measured mental ability it was just not fair, and not very meaningful, to compare, say, people born in 1910 with those born in 1940, for they had had different educational and work experience, and the care of their health throughout their lives had been dependent on the state of medical knowledge and public health at the time. Those born later had had a much better deal.

But however much more enlightened about the real facts of ageing modern professional people are (the more competent ones, that is – for we will always have backwoodsmen who did their training umpteen years ago, and refuse to accept new ideas), the public stereotype of older people is still conditioned by the prejudices of long ago. Indeed, it is often the older generation themselves who cling to the myths they learnt in their childhood and who will not wake up to the realities of life. Mental abilities change with ageing, and some problems have to be tackled in a different way, but these abilities do not have to deteriorate. You may have to work harder, in some ways, to maintain your accustomed standards of performance, although you may become more able in some respects as you age. The choice is yours: you can become a 'poor old thing' if you like.

THE TWO APPROACHES

It is not to be denied that some types of memory and general mental performance do decline with age if we measure what might be termed the end product, and this is confirmed by studying the same individuals over time longitudinally. The argument is about why the decline takes place. The two main positions are:

A. To regard such decline as being mainly the result of a lowering of the physical efficiency of the brain processes with age, which is comparable to other degenerative processes like loss of hair, wrinkling of the skin and lowering of the resistance to disease;

B. To regard the lowering of working efficiency as being due mainly to the brain becoming too complex in its organization and the memory-banks over-stocked with material that is not always well organized.

Ageing is not a sudden process that begins at a certain age. Some mental abilities seem to decline at a remarkably early age, and it is difficult to understand why. Most brilliant mathematicians do their best work before the age of 30 and afterwards there may be some decline, whereas as noted earlier, the great violinist Pablo Casals continued to practise daily in his nineties, and believed that he was improving thereby. It may be that for various mental abilities there is a peak age of efficiency when the relevant system of the brain is just complex enough, and further complexity can only lead to lowered performance.

One ability that can improve with age is the use of language. I do not mean fluency of speaking, a matter that involves muscular efficiency, but the effective use of language and a wide knowledge of vocabulary.

REMEMBERING TO DO THINGS IN THE FUTURE

Are you worried, not so much about your memory for things past, but concerning what you must do in the future?

I knew a man who was in pain with toothache all one week and was much looking forward to his dental appointment on the Friday afternoon. The pain was of that kind that comes and goes, and he was counting on his dentist to get rid of it once and for all. On the Friday morning it appeared to have gone, and he meant to ask his dentist about this mysterious coming and going, but later in the day a sharp twinge of pain reminded him that he had entirely forgotten to keep the dental appointment even though it was there in his diary and he had been looking forward to it all week! The temporary cessation of pain had defused the mechanism governing future action. It was as though the wished-for event was already in the past.

Professor Baddeley, a well-known expert on memory, tells an amusing story about himself. He had agreed to join a panel of experts discussing memory for a live radio programme that was to be broadcast one morning at the local station. The morning came and he proceeded with his normal routine, entirely forgetting this appointment. He was looking at the morning paper, wondering what was on TV that evening, when the thought of television reminded him of radio, and he realized with horror that at that moment he should be at the broadcasting station answering listeners' phone-in questions about memory! He rushed there in his car and was in time to join the panel for the summing up, murmuring excuses about the awful conditions of traffic jams.

Professor Baddeley was by no means elderly at that time and could not be labelled an 'Absent-minded Old Professor'. He was just a very busy man accomplishing a great deal of work by sticking to a certain routine, and this radio appointment was outside his normal working procedure. A Freudian might say that he didn't want to fulfil the obligation and so forgot it, but this psychodynamic explanation for such forgetting is hardly adequate, because he did go there after all, and caused himself a considerable amount of embarrassment.

Many psychologists believe that these lapses in what they call the 'prospective memory' are more frequent in later life, but I am not entirely convinced by their evidence. They have devised tests that can be applied in the laboratory, and such tests have demonstrated that when groups of older people are compared with younger groups, the old do worse. In one test the instruction occurs 'Underline the word fox when you next encounter it', and 'In three minutes time put a tick in the margin to show how far you have got.' Thus you have to hold in mind a number of future actions that are to be performed, as well as coping with the ongoing test items.

Now comes the paradox: in real life situations it is younger people who really do worse in matters concerning prospective memory. It is they who most often fail to keep appointments, and arrive too late to catch trains. They return their library books too late, and forget to do things at the proper time. This is more than an impression formed on a few anecdotal incidents: it is the result of formal studies of actual behaviour, and even when those studied have had a financial incentive for doing the right thing at the right time, younger people tend to do worse.

Freud discussed the problem in his typically cynical way, and referring to failures to observe future social engagements punctiliously, he wrote: 'In these cases the motive is usually a large amount of unavowed contempt for other people.' Some people would say much the same - that 'the young' are just lacking in proper manners. (This is said by every older generation!) The main cause of the observed difference in real life is probably that most people are well aware of the gross defect in prospective memory that is supposed to come with ageing, and take active steps to prevent it. As they grow older and retirement approaches, and have to cope with the increasing demands that their jobs and social lives make of them, they learn to depend more and more on diaries, marked calendars and formalized routines so that they make relatively few lapses. If we see ourselves as being in danger of becoming the 'Absent-minded Old Professor' this bogy spurs us on to take special precautions. As we age we make more and more use of prostheses such as spectacles, false teeth, walking sticks and hearing aids; diaries and other forward planning devices are just another form of prostheses to aid our over-burdened memory-bank.

What is so interesting about prospective memory is that it is quite different from other forms of memory storage. When we think of memory, we conceive a bank of past impressions that can normally be retrieved at will. But prospective memory involves continuous activity in the brain which will respond to future events that we refer to as 'cues', and respond as with a triggered mechanism. Alternatively, the response may not be triggered by any external event, but by the mere passage of time, the brain acting like an alarm clock. In the case of the man that I described earlier who missed his dental appointment, the cessation of pain de-fused, as it were, the forward looking mechanism so the appropriate action was never taken when the time came.

In the case of the professor who failed to fulfil his engagement at the broadcasting station, he was so dominated by his usual busy and demanding daily routine that it took an external cue to remind him.

There is a serious neurotic illness in which the sufferers become so dominated by, and obsessed with, the tasks which they have to perform in the future, that life becomes a misery. They cannot relax and enjoy the present because they are frantically preparing for the future. This condition is known as 'obsessional neurosis' – the prospective memory seems to go haywire.

THE CASE OF PHINEAS GAGE

A small amount of obsessionalism makes people very reliable workers, and in their social life they will always turn up very promptly for appointments and fulfil their obligations very conscientiously. Their friends regard them as fuss-pots. Such a one was Phineas Gage, an American workman who was promoted to be a foreman because of his dependability and devotion to duty. In 1848 he suffered a curious accident: an iron rod was shot right through the front part of his head thus destroying part of the frontal lobes of his brain. He recovered very well from this serious accident and regained his health, but he was a changed man. He became lazy and undependable, and took no thought for the future. Eventually his employers had to sack him. This event is of great historical importance because it indicated to those studying the brain that the frontal lobes were the part that is concerned with thinking ahead, what has become known as prospective memory.

In the 1930s there began an era of treating obsessional neurosis in its extreme form (patients being driven crazy with morbid worry) by 'leucotomy'. This involved cutting through the nerves of the frontal lobes surgically, thus preventing the extremes of over-activity. It was always a controversial procedure; it benefited some patients by making their lives livable, but it rendered some patients rather cabbage-like. Later this practice was replaced by the less drastic procedure that is in use today: the passing of an electric shock through the whole, or part of the frontal area of the brain. It is still a controversial treatment, but it is certainly beneficial in some cases.

So what do you do if you are concerned that your prospective memory is letting you down? Well, people of all ages are coping with this very sensibly by the use of diaries, forward planners, and even electronic devices that give a bleep at certain times when you have to ring your friend, go and see the boss, or take a cake out of the oven. You should not hesitate to use such devices; just as you accept that you wear spectacles if you need to – do not regard them as the badge of decrepit age! There is the old-fashioned device of tying a knot in your handkerchief, but you may discover it only hours after the critical time has passed, or take it out of your pocket and say 'What on earth does this knot mean ? I simply can't remember!' A useful tip is to remind yourself of some very, very important engagement by sticking a tiny adhesive label on the face of your watch and write, say 'J3' on it. You frequently look at your watch during the day and you will see this label, and every time you will be reminded that you must meet Jane at 3 o'clock.

ABSENT-MINDEDNESS

I have referred to the 'Absent-minded Old Professor' who
forgets to fulfil engagements in the future, but you should note that
there is a significant difference between failure of the prospective
memory and absent-mindedness. The latter term literally means
that your mind is absent from what you are doing at the present
moment.

You are very much absorbed in thinking about some problem, and
you absent-mindedly pour hot water into the milk jug instead of the
teapot; you offer cornflakes to the cat instead of the baby; you go to
your bedroom after tea to change your dress and find that you are
beginning to put on your nightgown; you go to the kitchen to fetch
something, but when you get there you begin to clean the sink instead of fetching the butter. These are examples of absent-minded
behaviour.

   Absent-mindedness is a very curious phenomenon that arises
from your capacity to carry out two unrelated things at the same
time. If you drive a car you are carrying out a skilled task of
manipulating the controls in response to your observation of the
traffic conditions, yet at the same time you may be carrying on an

animated conversation with a friend in the passenger seat. This wonderful capacity for doing two things at once is possible because many of our skills are over-learnt and almost automatic. You trust yourself to get on with the job of manipulating the controls in response to the traffic conditions, while you fix your attention on your friend while you try to convince her that your son is a fit person to marry her daughter. Absent-mindedness is manifest when you arrive at your destination and find that you have taken the accustomed route to your office and not to your friend's house as you intended. The effects of absent-mindedness can be very worrying. You cannot find your keys – where on earth can they be? Eventually you find them in the bathroom cupboard where you put the new tube of tooth-paste. You cannot find the unopened letters that came at breakfast-time; eventually they are discovered on the shelf under the telephone, and you then recall that the telephone rang as you were carrying them to the breakfast table.

Absent-minded acts are due not to failures of memory, but to your having too many problems on your mind. They cannot be prevented by use of the usual sort of memory aids that are useful in coping with possible failure in the prospective memory, but you can guard against the effects of them by making your general routine of living more structured, eg, by keeping your keys always hanging on the hook in the hall, and never putting them down in various places.

4

THE TIP- OF-THE-TONGUE PHENOMENON

This is such an interesting and puzzling phenomenon that it deserves a chapter to itself. There is some reason to think that it is more common in later life, but no one is very clear about how much it is related to ageing.

An elderly woman remarked to a psychologist, 'If you want to study something really important, find out why I can't remember the name of my friend of 20 years when I go to introduce her.' But psychologists have not made a great deal of progress in studying this curious experience.

You try to think of the name of a person, a flower, a town – names that are perfectly well known to you, and to your surprise and frustration you find that it is just not available. You know that it is stored in your memory, for you have used it many times, but somehow it just will not come – it is 'on the tip of the tongue.' Sometimes it is not the name of a person, an object or a place, but an abstract word like 'cantankerous', and it eludes you when you want to use it in speech or writing. You don't block every time you try to use the word, just sometimes.

One of the very curious thing about the tip-of-the-tongue (TOT) blockage is that if you leave the search alone for a while, the word will often 'pop up' in your mind when you are thinking of something else, and this appears to happen for no particular reason. Indeed, when you are dealing with lists of names it may be a wise strategy to leave alone any recalcitrant names that will not come to mind immediately. If you carry on with the list it is quite likely that you will suddenly remember the missing name. It is as though a search process has continued to operate, scanning the memory-bank, without your being consciously aware of it.

The analogy of a word processor may be helpful from time to time, but always bear in mind the fact that the brain is not a computer. When these machines were first designed, a lot of processes were incorporated that are very similar to brain functions. Those who use word processors in their homes or offices will know that although they are very much like typewriters, what is typed appears on an illuminated screen and is stored in the machine's 'memory'. If the user wishes to find a particular word in a document that has been typed, this can be achieved by pressing a key marked 'find' and typing the desired word. What happens then is that the marker scans the whole
document, line by line, until it comes to the word that is needed, and highlights it. If it is a short document, the wanted word is soon found, but with a lengthy document the scanning process may take some time. This is analogous to what happens when you try to retrieve a particular name or word that is stored in your memory; generally the search is almost instantaneous, but occasionally you get a TOT blockage and the scanning process is lengthy. You may not get the desired word for hours, days, and sometimes never.

In trying to remember the names of two past colleagues I had to wait a year for one of them to come to mind, and I have not yet retrieved the other. If it were important I could easily look it up, but as it isn't, I am content to wait to see if it will ever emerge.

The memory-banks of older people are often rather over-loaded because of their long lives' experience, it is natural that the TOT phenomenon will be more frequent, and that the scanning process will take longer; it has nothing to do with any supposed brain deterioration – it's just that they know too much!

BREAKING THE TOT BLOCKAGE
There is no complete answer to breaking the TOT blockage but, if you are prepared to follow the instructions given, you will master some useful techniques and have a greater insight into how your memory operates.

The Definitions Test

If you are willing, I now propose to create some TOT blockages in you and let you struggle with them, then show you how to call to mind words that you already know but obstinately remain on the tip of your tongue. First take a piece of paper and write the numbers 1 to 20 in a vertical column. Below are some definitions of objects and words. Write down on your paper the objects and words defined, using one word only in each case.

1. A stringed instrument like a guitar or banjo, but strummed, not plucked.
2. To obliterate, delete, wipe out, cancel.
3. Continuous rapid talk, twaddle.
4. To pacify, appease, reconcile, placate.
5. A very small grassy mound or hillock.
6. Potential, not yet manifest.
7. A corpse, said to be revived by witchcraft.
8. Stubborn and hard, inexorable.
9. A man's soft, low-crowned hat, rather like a trilby.
10. To alleviate, mitigate, ease, make less painful.
11. A Jonah, a person, or thing, that brings bad luck.
12. To flatter basely and undeservedly.
13. A Russian collective farm.
14. Successful, happy, prosperous.
15. The compass of actions, or confines of a district.
16. Abstruse, deep, profound, little known.
17. Scanty in size or number, extremely small, diminutive.
18. A vertical bar dividing the lights in a Gothic window.
19. Supposed, reputed.
20. To liberate, to set free from slavery.

If you are very learned you may have defined each one, but if you think you know a word but a TOT blockage prevents you from writing it, put a tick beside it. When you have done all you can, consider the following: these are the initial letters of all the words defined, and with their help see if you can break the TOT blockage in some or all cases – U, E, W, C, T, L, Z, O, F, P, J, A, K, F, A, R, E, M, P, M. Go ahead and write the words in. Some of the words towards the bottom of the list are rather unusual and may have defeated you; a complete list is given in the *Appendix* at the end of this chapter.

You have probably noted that when a TOT blockage is released, you get a little glow of satisfaction, and that is why some people enjoy doing crossword puzzles. Their purpose is to create TOT blockages, and then allow people to release them as they solve clue after clue.

The Geography Test

If you want to attempt another practical exercise take a piece of paper and write the numbers 1 to 20 in a vertical column and against each number write the names of the capital cities of the following countries:

1. Turkey.
2. Romania.
3. Colombia.
4. Thailand.
5. Venezuela.
6. Australia.
7. Syria.
8. Sudan.
9. Tibet.
10. Nicaragua.
11. Uruguay.
12. Cyprus.
13. Kenya.
14. Norway.
15. Equador.
16. Saudi Arabia.
17. Burma.
18. Bulgaria.
19. South Korea.
20. Cameroon.

If you have a fairly average knowledge of geography you will find that these countries fall into three categories:

A. You know the name of the capital city – so write it down against the appropriate number.

B. You really know the name of the capital city, but it is on the tip of your tongue and you cannot recall it now. For these cases put a tick against the number.

C. You don't know, and you are sure that you never have known the name of the capital city, so put a cross against the numbers of such countries.

Don't read on until you have filled in all you can.

You should now have a column of names of cities, ticks and crosses and you will be ready to take the first step in removing the TOT blockages. Look at the cities that you have already written down and you will note that they are in alphabetical order down the column (two or more cities may share the same initial letter). All the cities are in alphabetical order, although some letters of the alphabet are omitted. Does this help you? With this knowledge perhaps you can fill in one or two more cities. When you come to the end of your patience, have a look at the following list of initial letters and you will probably be able to put a name after each one of the ticks: A, B, B, B, C, C, D, K, L, M, M, N, N, O, Q, R, R, S, S, Y. If you are still wracked with frustration, turn to the *Appendix* at the end of this chapter where you will find the names of the capital cities printed upside-down.

In using alphabetical order to assist you in breaking a TOT blockage you are making use of an existing structure that is firmly fixed in your memory. Anyone who has never learned the alphabetical order (as I believe some children do not in modern schools) would be lacking in this structure and unable to benefit from it. Because alphabetical order is very fundamental to the storing of words, you can think of pigeon-holing each word, and when you wish to retrieve it, going to the appropriate one of the 26 pigeon-holes to scan its contents. Thus, when you know the initial letter of any word that is temporarily eluding your memory, the search process is much easier. Words are of course classified in many more ways as well as alphabetical order (eg. whether they refer to animal, vegetable or mineral) and the more you know about a word the quicker your retrieval process will be.

You are not always conscious of what factors are helping or hindering you in the search for a word that is blocked. It seems obvious that an unconscious search process is going on while you are engaged in thinking of other things, and what byways and corridors of the mind (if I may use such figurative terms) are being travelled are quite unknown.

So what goes wrong when you have the TOT experience? The categorization and cross-referencing system in our brains is of almost unbelievable complexity, and it is a wonder the TOT phenomenon does not occur more frequently. What happens is that in the scanning process the search gets mis-routed because words have so many, many connections.

THE UGLY SISTERS

The term 'ugly sister' refers to the Prince's search for Cinderella, the girl whom he had met at the ball, and whose glass slipper he retained. It will be remembered that the Prince had first to test the two ugly sisters to see if the slipper fitted them before he finally came to Cinderella, the object of his search. Psychologists have therefore given the fanciful name of 'ugly sister' to a word that comes to mind and gets in the way when you are searching for a word that is on the tip of your tongue. Every time you try to retrieve X it eludes you, and Y comes to mind. Often Y seems to be not in anyway similar to the word you are searching for: you try to remember the name of a piece of music by Beethoven, and 'steak pie' comes to mind.

Let me describe my own experience with a word that re-peatedly eluded me for a long period of time. I repeatedly re-learnt it, but time after time it remained on the tip of my tongue when I wanted to use it.

The word was 'hydrangea', a garden flower, but every time I tried to retrieve it the word 'aquilegia' came to mind. This was the 'ugly sister'. It was also a garden flower. A repeated block for certain words is not uncommon, particularly when the 'ugly sister' is similar in some way to the missing word. Eventually I got over this blockage on 'hydrangea' by realizing the significance of 'aquilegia'. It was my confusion between the Greek and the Latin, subjects I had learned at school at an elementary level. In Greek hydra = water; in Latin aqua = water; for some reason the Latin was getting in the way of the Greek. Once I had realized this I had no more TOT experiences with the name 'hydrangea'.

A second example may illustrate the means I have used for getting over TOT blockages which do not seem to have any cause that I can discover. For quite a long period I had difficulty in remembering the name of the well-known actor W C Fields. I had seen him in a number of films and knew quite a lot about him, but often when I tried to remember his name nothing would come – not even an 'ugly sister'. He was a very outgoing and rumbustious character and addicted to drink. He often carried a bottle of whiskey around with him and referred to it as his 'pineapple juice'.

Eventually I devised a means of recalling this actor's name by pondering on him and relating him to Shakespeare's character Falstaff, whom he resembled in many ways: he loved drink and was a boastful liar. I remembered that in *King Henry V* Mistress Quickly tells of the death of Falstaff and says 'a babbled of green fields'. For some reason this association was significant to me and I never forgot Fields' name again.

THE PUZZLE OF BLOCKED RECALL

No specialist in memory has yet come up with a really satisfactory explanation of the TOT phenomenon, although it has been described by many writers. It raises the question of how you normally recall a piece of information that is stored in the long-term memory. As mentioned before, words are not stored in isolation but in a vast network of interconnected neurones. We don't know the basis of the storage; presumably electrical currents as well as brain chemicals are involved in buzzing activity between the neurones, and when you learn a new piece of information, say, the name of a new actor, this name is stored in association with a network that is concerned with the names of other actors, the names of plays and films, playwrights, theatres and all things concernig the world of drama. If the new actor's name was 'Churchill' it might have weak associations with politics, World War II, etc, and many other networks concerning whatever personal associations you have with the name.

It might be that you wished to recall the name of the young actor who took the part of Laertes in a recent production of *Hamlet*; a search process would then start in the stage network, and several associated networks as well, and quickly (or not so quickly) the brain activity would home in on the name of Churchill.

What I have just written is speculation, but it is informed speculation. But what happens when in the search process a connection with a largely irrelevant network is activated? Earlier I mentioned that in trying to remember the name of a piece of music by Beethoven a TOT blockage might occur, and all that would come to mind might be 'steak pie' – a very bizarre 'ugly sister'. Just how and why it pops up is a complete mystery, for you have no sort of map of the organization of your neural networks. It is as though when searching for a book on music in the library, using the usual library cross-reference system, you are directed to a shelf of books concerning cookery.

But not many efforts to remember go so grossly wrong. The TOT experience rarely occurs. Generally any blockage is of short duration, and the right word reveals itself quite soon. A study of TOT experiences teaches us something about the retrieval of memories – that it takes time. Normally the search process is almost instantaneous, as otherwise you could not speak at all, but if you listen to a person speaking English whose native language is some other tongue, you will hear the pauses, sometimes filled with the sound 'er' as the search process is slowed. 'In my country – er – we have a custom of – er – sleeping in the – er – afternoon.' A few people have the habit of peppering their speech in their native language with the sound 'er'. I knew a psychology professor who was very nervous of public speaking, and when he gave a talk for the BBC they first had to record it on tape, and then snip out all the 'ers' so that when it was broadcast it sounded quite fluent.

Nervousness will slow up speech. Presumably the normal flow of brain processes, and hence speech, is being interrupted by thoughts such as 'Am I making a fool of myself? I'm making mistakes all the time! I'll never get through this ordeal!'

THE FREUDIAN EXPLANATION

An ingenious explanation of the TOT phenomenon comes from the psychoanalytic school. Freud himself gives a long discussion of how he blocked on the name of the painter Signorelli, and substituted two other painters names as what we would now call 'ugly sisters'. His analysis of this case led him to believe it was due to repression of personal associations concerning 'death and sexuality'. The psycho-analytic suggestion is that in the process of searching for a name, a memory trace may be activated that evokes an unpleasant emotional response because it touches on 'repressed' memories, and this causes a blockage and perhaps the substitution of another name that is in some way connected but emotionally neutral.

I have given the example of how I repeatedly forgot the name of W C Fields, and a Freudian explanation might well go along the following lines. The actor's initials are W C, and water-closets are often associated with emotional conflicts in early childhood that arise out of toilet training. According to psychoanalytic theory, such early conflicts are often 'repressed' and you do not remember them in later life. Could it be that my hidden associations with the actors initials were responsible for the blockage? Even after I had read it again and again the TOT mechanism still made the name elude me, and perhaps only a psychoanalytic recovery of the original childhood experiences would finally release me from this inhibition.

But I might object to this explanation by pointing out that I never had any difficulty with remembering the name of an American psychologist W C Coe – does this contradict the explanation? Here a super-ingenious psychoanalyst might suggest that the surname might also be involved: that Fields in association with W C might remind me of some emotionally traumatic experiences in early childhood concerned with using fields for excretory purposes instead of the W C.

I do not wish to make fun of psychoanalytic explanations, but in general they have the drawback that they can never be proved or disproved. Anyone with sufficient ingenuity can think them up, but it is doubtful if they are really valid. The same might be said of my attempted explanation for my blocking on the name 'hydrangea' in terms of a confusion between the Greek and Latin word for 'water'. I have no proof of its correctness, and it may be quite mistaken. The fact that I got rid of the blockage by this analysis, may simply be due to the fact that I worked on the problem and created new connections with the name, even though my reasoning may have been faulty. In the same way, a psychoanalytic explanation may remove a blockage, even though it may be quite far-fetched.

One objection to the Freudian explanation of the TOT phenomenon is that it offers no explanation for the fact that such blockages are more common in later life. I think the more plausible explanation is simply that the older you get the more over-stuffed and complex your memory-banks become because of your greater experience of life. It is a horrid thing to slay a beautiful theory with an ugly fact, but the more mundane explanation seems more probable to me.

THE HYPNOTIC TOT
The whole subject of hypnosis is still shrouded in mystery in the minds of most lay people, but in more recent decades of experimental work that has been carried out, largely by American psychologists, it has become more understandable. We now know a great deal about

hypnosis although it is still a lively battleground for rival schools of psychology. Most knowledgeable people are now agreed that it is not so mysterious a phenomenon as was once thought. What can be achieved by means of hypnosis fits in very well with accepted theories of learning and memory.

It will be helpful to give a dictionary definition of hypnosis so you know what we are discussing:

Hypnosis *is a state that resembles normal sleep but differs in being induced by the suggestions of the hypnotizer with whom the hypnotized subject remains in rapport and responsive to his suggestions*
Webster's Dictionary

The term is sometimes used loosely in medical writing to refer to the state induced by the so-called 'hypnotic' (that is, soporific) drugs. As used in psychology, hypnosis has nothing to do with a drugged state.

The TOT phenomenon can be produced by suggesting to a hypnotized subject that after hypnosis a certain word will be forgotten, that it cannot be retrieved from the memory until a 'releasing cue' is given. It may also be suggested that the subject will have no memory at all for having been given this prohibitive suggestion. The releasing cue, which has been fixed in hypnosis, may be some sign that the experimenter makes, such as taking off his spectacles, or simply saying 'Now you can remember' – then the TOT blockage is broken.

The creation of a TOT blockage by means of hypnotic suggestion is not really a very strange phenomenon. The occurrence of the TOT experience in normal waking life without anything obviously precipitating it, is surely just as strange. Hypnosis has been very useful in exploring the complexities of memory, and there is one interesting experiment that demonstrates what might be called a TOT for the source of information. This is known as the generation of 'source amnesia': a subject is given new information which is retained, but he or she has no memory for when or how it was acquired.

The experiment generally proceeds like this: a subject is hypnotized and then given various pieces of unusual factual information, eg, the height of Mount Kenya; the population of Wigan; the exact age of a senior politician. Before terminating the hypnosis by 'wakening' the subject, the experimenter says that this information will be remembered, but that there will be no memory for how it was acquired. After hypnosis there is conversation, perhaps with several people, and the discussion leads to topics about which the specialized knowledge has been imparted. Subjects find, perhaps to their surprise, that they have exact knowledge pertaining to the height of

Mount Kenya, etc. When asked how and when such knowledge was learned, the question is shrugged off. When it is explained to the subject just what was said in hypnosis, memory comes flooding back – the TOT blockage is broken.

You may wonder whether these strange effects are not just the result of the subject play-acting to please the hypnotist. This is a legitimate question and it deserves a careful answer.

No one can be hypnotized against their will; in agreeing to be hypnotized and going along with the trance-inducing process, the subject abandons the normal critical and evaluative attitude that characterizes normal waking consciousness, and lets the suggestions of the hypnotist act upon the imagination, so that what is suggested strongly determines ongoing thought processes. Thus the normal process of retrieving memories is interfered with, and some memories may become temporarily inaccessible, both within hypnosis and immediately afterwards.

From the records of hypnosis sessions long ago, and earlier in this century when experimenters were less tender-minded about their subjects' feelings and rights, we know that quite drastic manipulations of subjects' memories and emotions were achieved in a manner that would be considered unethical today. Memories for the

commission of imaginary crimes were induced by suggestion, and the guilt induced by such memories produced emotional upsets that were recordable by physiological changes. Such facts go against the simplistic view that hypnosis is all a matter of play-acting.

This is all relevant to the previous discussion about the implanting of false memories of being abused in childhood by means of extensive suggestive psychotherapy with vulnerable people, which often does involve hypnosis. It is not only a matter of blotting out true memories by techniques similar to the induction of the TOT effect by hypnosis, but of creating 'ugly sisters' which are built up as though they were true memories. Our memories are very vulnerable

to changes and manipulations, and the TOT phenomenon is an
excellent example of this vulnerability.

DO INCREASED TOT EXPERIENCES WITH AGEING
INDICATE BRAIN DETERIORATION?

'Nominal aphasia' is a jargon term for the inability to remember
names that is one of the results of brain damage due to violence,
poisoning, or disease. It is natural that older people, when they
sense an increase in their TOT experiences, should fear that it is
due to deterioration of the brain. But although the TOT phenomenon mimics such aphasia, it differs from it in a number of ways.
Brain tissue does not heal like other body tissue, so people never
fully recover from the effects of serious damage to the brain. The
boxer who is aphasic because of repeated blows to the head (his
condition is referred to as being 'punchy') will never regain his
normal mental powers. By contrast, memories that appear to be
lost through the TOT phenomenon can be fully and permanently
recovered.

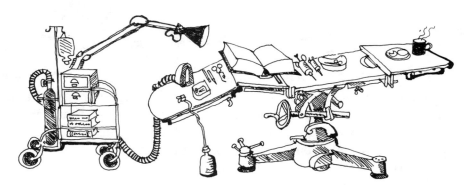

TOT episodes increase in frequency at certain periods of our lives.
Schoolchildren suffer from them when frantically trying to make up
for lost time in revising for exams, as do medical students when
they struggle to transfer the whole of Gray's Anatomy to their
long-term memory-banks. I suffer from something like the TOT

effect in my untidy office when I have failed to keep up with my filing, and frantically search for mislaid documents in the wrong place. If you wish to avoid repeated TOT frustrations you must be more methodical in your reading, writing, talking and life style. This is counsel that is easy to give, but difficult to follow. If you have a lively mind and a great range of interests in later life, surely you should be prepared to endure TOT experiences as a small price to pay for living life to the full intellectually and enjoying yourself?

The mechanism of the TOT phenomenon has never been explained fully, nor must we expect an adequate explanation until psychologists, neurologists and other scientists have found out a lot more about the working of the brain. All that we can do is to make various informed speculations and guesses as to what sorts of mechanisms are at work. Some knowledge is better than no knowledge – it is now known, for instance, that older people are more prone to have TOT experiences than young adults and the sort of words they block on are different. Older people block more on names of people, places and objects, but young adults block more on abstract nouns, adjectives and verbs, a difference that may relate to the fact that in later life people have rather richer vocabularies in which to express themselves, but their memory-banks are stuffed with so many names of people, places, and objects.

The study of the TOT phenomena advances our understanding of the whole nature of memory storage and retrieval, and suggests reasons why it is more common in later life. Even with our modest understanding we can suggest techniques for overcoming the frustration of TOT blockages.

APPENDIX TO CHAPTER 4

Anwers to the tests given on pages 67 and 68

DEFINITION OF WORDS   Test on page 67

1 Ukelele, 2 Efface, 3 Waffle, 4 Conciliate, 5 Tussock, 6 Latent,
7 Zombie, 8 Obdurate, 9 Fedora, 10 Palliate, 11 Jinx, 12 Adulate,
13 Kolkhoz, 14 Felicitous, 15 Ambit, 16 Recondite, 17 Exiguous,
18 Mullion, 19 Putative, 20 Manumit.

CAPITAL CITIES   Test on page 68

1 Ankara, 2 Bucharest, 3 Bogota, 4 Bangkok, 5 Caracas, 6 Canberra,
7 Damascus, 8 Khartoum, 9 Lhasa, 10 Managua, 11 Montevideo,
12 Nicosia, 13 Nairobi, 14 Oslo, 15 Quito, 16 Riyadh, 17 Rangoon,
18 Sophia, 19 Seoul, 20 Yaounde.

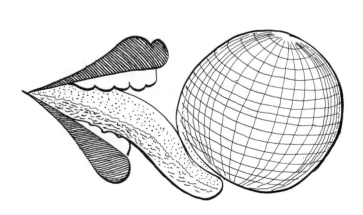

5

GIMMICKS FOR REMEMBERING: MNEMONICS

There are lots of books on sale which set out to improve your memory, and they generally give a good deal of space to mnemonics, the gimmicks that help the learning of all sorts of pieces of information, such as the dates of historical happenings and the colours of the rainbow spectrum in order. Most of these books are targeted at students who are cramming for examinations and whose memory-banks are temporarily over-loaded with a vast mass of factual information. Most of you will never need to take another exam-ination and your interest in memory is not that of overburdening your minds with lists of facts. It is useful, however, to take a look at these gimmicks for the light they throw on the mechanisms of memory and how you can tackle problems in real life.

A lot of the techniques depend upon attaching newly learnt material to structures that already exist in your long-term memory, so that retrieval of the newly memorized material is rendered easy. You could make a great deal of use of mnemonics in your daily life, but on the whole it would be boring and unnecessary. You could, for instance, commit to memory a long list of items to be bought, and errands to be fulfilled before going on a shopping expedition in the morning. But why bother? It is easier to make out a shopping list.

WHAT ARE MNEMONICS?
The word 'mnemonics' (pronounced nemonics) derives from the Greek goddess of memory, Mnemosyne, and hence its strange spelling. Mnemonic techniques have certainly been in use for over 2500 years, and many books on memory begin by relating a tall tale about how the Greek poet Simonides invented 'the place method' (called by the Romans the method of loci) but I will not bother you with this story.

Essentially mnemonics are ways of associating words and ideas together in a memorable manner, and they can be roughly divided into visual and verbal methods. For instance, if you wanted to associate the word 'carrot' with 'justice', you could do it in your minds eye by imagining a Justice of the Peace with a carrot for a nose – a striking image which you could easily remember. If you wished to remember the association verbally, you could make up a memorable sentence such as, 'J Ps use the whip and the carrot in keeping the peace.'

THE PLACE METHOD

This was used by both Greek and Roman orators for remembering a long list of items that might have little connection with each other but had to be dealt with in a speech. They imagined a room that was very familiar to them containing a number of well-remembered features that could be easily visualized in the mind's eye. Thus if the speech was first to deal with the war with the Goths, then go on to taxing the plebs, proceeding to discuss the disastrous olive harvest . . . and so forth, a Goth warrior might be visualized at the entrance to the room, followed by a typical plebeian shopkeeper sitting in the hearth turning out his empty pockets, while on his left stood a cracked jar of olives leaking oil on to the pile of logs. As he proceeded round the room in imagery the orator would thus encounter point after point that he intended to make, and all in proper order. He would not skip from the Goths to the olives and then back to the plebs.

If you would like to try it for yourself, write down a typical shopping list, then just visualise your own sitting room, and walking round it, note whatever objects you choose – the clock on the mantel-piece, the blue vase on the table, the photograph of your son on the bookcase, and so on. This is a fixed image in your memory. Now consider your shopping list to be learned: balance the loaf of bread on the clock, wrap toilet paper round the blue vase, place a bottle of gin beside your son's face, and proceed to decorate each object in the room with what is on your shopping list. The more absurd and striking the juxtaposition of the objects the better.

I am not going to suggest that you now go out shopping, since this is only an illustrative test. Close the book and distract yourself with something else for a few minutes, and when you have had a rest, try to write down the shopping list on another piece of paper, travelling round your sitting room in your visual imagery as you do so. How successful were you? I should point out that this method greatly favours those of us who are natural visualizers.

WHY BOTHER?

As I said earlier, in real life why bother? Why not do the sensible thing and take your list with you when you go out shopping and tick off the items as you buy them?

Books never seem to consider this possibility, probably because they have students in mind – students are not allowed to take scraps of paper into examinations, and when they are caught doing so they are for it! So they depend on mnemonics such as:

Richard of York Gave Battle In Vain to remind them of the order the colours come in the light spectrum (Red, Orange, Yellow, Green, Blue, Indigo, Violet), which may help in a physics examination.

And in a history examination:
In fourteen hundred and ninety-two
Columbus sailed the ocean blue.
– may be of help; unless, of course, in the heat of examination nervousness it comes out as:
In fifteen hundred and ninety-two
Columbus sailed the ocean blue.

– which sounds just as good, but the examiner will mark the student down for appearing to believe that the memorable voyage did not take place until the sixteenth century. This is the danger of depending upon mnemonics! You may well ask why the classical orator did not simply write down his significant points on a piece of paper as a modern speaker would do? Merely because it was not the done thing – he was like an actor, and words were supposed to spring from his heart without the need for artificial prompts.

I did not describe and illustrate 'the place method' for fun, but for a very practical purpose. Consider what happened when you tried to apply this method (if you did) to your own shopping list. The items were in your short-term memory, and in order to store them in your long-term memory you worked on them, creating a visual image for each one and attaching it to a pre-existent image of something that was already well established in your long-term memory, an item in your sitting room.

One objection to your depending on a list written on a scrap of paper is that you might leave it behind on the hall table as you leave the house. I have done this more than once! But all was not lost; the mere act of writing the items down was working on them, and thereby transferring them from my short-term to my long-term memory. I could even remember the look of the scrawl on the back of an old envelope. It was certainly better than nothing.

THE PEGWORD METHOD

This is a method of using visual imagery and combining it with rhyming. It deals with turning numbers into concrete objects that can be visualized. Consider the standard list of rhymes:

One - bun	Six - sticks
Two - shoe	Seven - heaven
Three - tree	Eight - gate
Four - door	Nine - wine
Five - hive	Ten - hen

You can extend your private pegword list as far as you like – eleven - Devon; twelve - elf . . . etc. That is up to you.

This is simple and easy to learn; every number has an object that rhymes with it. While numbers are difficult to visualize as a mental picture, these objects are very easy. Have a go and learn the list; you will soon accomplish it, and then visualize each object – and make them your very own. The bun can be a Bath bun, a Chelsea bun, an iced bun, a bun showing many currants – let your fantasy rip and design your own special bun. And so go down the list. What kind of shoe are you going to imagine? What kind of tree? Once you have them firmly fixed in your mind, you can do things with combinations of numbers that were impossible before. For instance, our artist has illustrated the telephone number 101 238 906 by turning it into: hen-bun, shoe-tree-gate, wine-O-sticks

To use such a system efficiently you need to have a fair visual imagination, a facility that can certainly be cultivated, and a sufficiently playful and ingenious mind. And here I should state, that for general purposes in improving your powers of memory (quite apart from learning the tricks of mnemonics) you should do your best to cultivate a relaxed and adventurous attitude of mind; never reject any device for remembering things because it appears 'silly' or 'absurd'.

But to return to the telephone number you need to remember, do not be satisfied with our artist's pictorial rendering of it; use your own objects and think up as many striking connections as you can. Once you have formed a mental picture of any string of numbers you will never, never forget it, and if you are the type of person for whom this method is easy, you can get into the habit of substituting your objects for numbers, so that when Directory Inquiries give you a string of numbers, you immediately form a picture in your mind - a series of significant objects.

A PRACTICAL EXERCISE

The Pegword Method is not only useful for remembering numbers; it can be applied to remembering any string of words. Take a shopping list for instance – could you easily remember the following?

1. Sugar
2. Bleach
3. Matches
4. Coffee powder
5. Bread
6. Shoe polish
7. Cake
8. Tinned milk
9. Butter
10. Tea

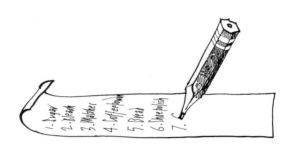

Note that to make it easy for you I have included just 10 items (as in the Pegword list) and they are all concrete objects so that you can form mental pictures of them. To convince yourself, try looking at the list, and make a mental picture of each item and attach it in your imagery to an image of the appropriate pegword. Thus the sugar will be attached to a bun (easy!), the bleach to a shoe, the matches to a tree, etc. When you think you have made all the associations in your mental imagery, try closing the book and writing down the list

Remember what I said earlier ? Why bother to do this when it is so easy to write a shopping list on paper? But the purpose of this and similar exercises, is to teach you how your memory works, and to get you to discover more about your own particular strengths and weaknesses. Do you remember things better by using visual imagery ?

Having got thus far in the book you have probably discovered that you have got a much better memory than you thought you had when you started it.

So far, in discussing applications of the Pegword list we have been dealing with concrete objects that are easy to visualize, packets of sugar, bottles of bleach and boxes of matches. But what about abstract concepts such as beauty, truth and justice? Can those concepts be treated likewise? Think back to our Roman orator who had to mention all sorts of abstract matters in his speech and could not depend on a written list. What did he do? If you want to test yourself on this, (and some readers may continue to find this fun, while others will say 'Enough is enough!'), consider the following 10 concepts and try forming mental images of them that can be fitted to your own special Pegword list:

1. Justice
2. Violence
3. Beauty
4. Love
5. Industry
6. Reluctance
7. Forgiveness
8. Honour
9. Weakness
10. Betrayal

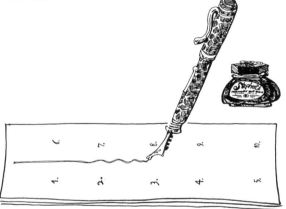

You could symbolize Justice by a bewigged judge (who is taking a bite out of your nice big bun), or Violence symbolized by your shoe kicking someone's shins. By now you should be adept at representing abstract qualities by concrete symbols. When you have done that in your head, close this book and **(i)** write down the double list of words showing the associations; **(ii)** try sketching the interaction of the words and the pegwords.

It does not matter how poor an artist you are, for no one need see your pictures, and for most people it really does help if they have their own drawings to remember.

LEARNING FOREIGN WORDS BY CONTEXT
AND BY VISUAL IMAGERY

If you have to learn difficult new material, say foreign words, or even the meaning of difficult words in your own language, visual imagery can be a great help. Some American psychologists investigated how best to teach students the meaning of a lot of rather abstruse words in order to raise their vocabulary level for the purpose of an examination. The students were taught by two different methods.

The context method. The difficult words were given together with a simple word of approximately the same meaning, plus an example of the use of each word in an appropriate context. Say the word was 'contumacious' – the students were told that it meant much the same as 'rebellious' and given the example of 'He was punished for being contumacious to his colonel.'

The keyword method. In the other method, they were given a 'keyword' that sounded much like the difficult word. Say the word was carlin (which means an old woman) the keyword was car. They were then instructed to form a visual image of the keyword in a sentence illustrating the meaning of the difficult word – here it would be an old woman driving a car. Thus the new word would be linked to its meaning by both its sound and a visual image.

The results of this experiment were surprising – when their memory for the meaning of the difficult words was tested later, those who used visual imagery of the keywords recalled 52% more definitions than those who used the context method.

If you would like to try this out on yourself, proceed as follows: **List A** and **List B** below have Japanese words; if you are familiar with the Japanese language this test will not work for you, but as it is unfamiliar to most Westerners this is a useful means of demonstrating this remarkable method of learning the vocabulary of a foreign language.

Read both **List A** and **List B** , and try to learn and remember the meanings of the Japanese words. **List A** has translations and examples of each word in context.

LIST A

SHOTAI = invitation   We received a SHOTAI to tea.

WARUI = wrong   Selling cocaine is WARUI.

NISEMONO = counterfeit   These antiques are really
                                                      NISEMONO.

SENKO = incense   We burn SENKO on the altar.

FUKUMU = to include   I wish to FUKUMU him in our
                                                      group.

KIROKU = record   We have no KIROKU of your
                                                      application.

UKETORI = receipt   I want a UKETORI for my cheque.

KOFUKU = happiness   The baby brought his mother great
                                                      KOFUKU.

DOJO = compassion   My DOJO was stirred by the sight
                                                      of the sick.

NEGIRU = to haggle   He wanted to NEGIRU over
                                                      the price.

List B also has Japanese words and their translations, followed by a sentence in which the English word is introduced, but gives information (entirely fictitious and fantastic!) which introduces the keyword and is followed by a sketch of it. The keyword sounds something like the pronunciation of the Japanese word and you should try hard to fix this sketch in your visual memory. So the Japanese word will be associated by both sound and vision.

LIST B

KOSHO = pepper
When *pepper* makes Japanese people sneeze they go 'a' – 'kosho'.

NEKO = a cat
Cats in Japan have long necks.

RODOSHA = a workman
The *workman* in Japan is typified by the road-worker

DADDAKO = a spoilt child
A *spoilt child* cries for his daddy too much

KOFU = miner
The *miner* coughs because of the coal dust.

GOGO = afternoon
In the *afternoon* factory workers are keen to go and go.

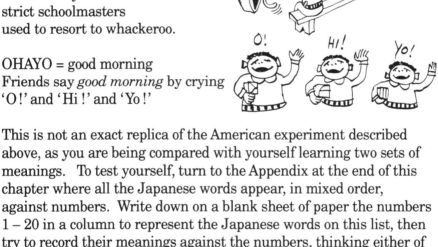

SHAKO = social intercourse
Social intercourse is the occasion
for much hand-shaking

ONNA = a woman
The Japanese *woman* is
the symbol of honour.

WAKARU = to understand
To make boys *understand*
strict schoolmasters
used to resort to whackeroo.

OHAYO = good morning
Friends say *good morning* by crying
'O!' and 'Hi!' and 'Yo!'

This is not an exact replica of the American experiment described above, as you are being compared with yourself learning two sets of meanings. To test yourself, turn to the Appendix at the end of this chapter where all the Japanese words appear, in mixed order, against numbers. Write down on a blank sheet of paper the numbers 1 – 20 in a column to represent the Japanese words on this list, then try to record their meanings against the numbers, thinking either of the context in which they appeared, or of the little sketches that you tried to memorize. When you have done this, and are sure that you can remember no more, turn back to **List A** and **List B** and compare your performance. I expect that you will have done rather better on **List B**, as here the meanings of the Japanese words were linked in your memory both by the sound of them and by your visual memory.

It would have been better, of course, if you had made the drawings yourself, for then it would have been your mental imagery rather than our artist's that would have created the little drawings.

VERBAL MNEMONICS

So far this chapter has concentrated on mnemonics that have depended principally on your visual imagery and memory, and from the time of the ancient Greeks visual images were emphasised in memory systems. The Roman orator Cicero maintained that 'The keenest of all our senses is the sense of sight, and that consequently perceptions received by the ears or by reflexion (thinking) can most easily be retained if they are also conveyed to our minds by the mediation of the eyes.'

Progress was made from the 16th century onwards in devising verbal mnemonics, largely for the purpose of teaching schoolchildren. The idea that education should consist principally of cramming children with facts and yet more facts, reached its peak in the 19th century, with an emphasis on rote learning. The Reverend Brayshaw wrote an amazing book which contained over 2000 historical dates and other snippets of knowledge about history, geography and the sciences which were to be memorized by means of rhymes . He also devised a curious number key by which the letters of the alphabet (consonants only) could be converted into numbers. He was, after the fashion of the time, simply concerned with history since the Norman conquest, and that being so, he could ignore the first two figures of dates as they occurred after 1066! His scheme, more for its interest than its utility (although you might like to use it) is given below:

1	2	3	4	5	6	7	8	9	0	00
B	D	G	J	L	M	P	R	T	W	St
C	F	H	K		N	Q		V	X	
			S			Z				

Once you have mastered the scheme you can do wonders with it and cram your head with all sorts of information provided you learn the Reverend Brayshaw's rhymes.

You make words by slipping in vowels between the consonants as required. Thus some dates of English kings are conveyed by the following:

By **MeN** near Hastings William gains the crown. (1066)

A **RaP** in Forest New brings Rufus down. (1087)

Gaul's **CoaSt** first Henry hates, whose son is drowned (1100)

Like **BeaGLe** Stephen fights with Maud renoun'd (1135)

The pupil had to be aware of the fact that the essential information was contained in the second or third word of the rhyme.

It is easy to deride such a cumbersome system of learning largely superfluous knowledge, but it was once accepted as perfectly normal by our ancestors. We should reflect that the origins of rhyming and expressing facts in metrical form were in pre-literate times when knowledge was handed down from one generation to the next in some form of verse that was thus rendered memorable. Verbal mnemonics are still a useful way of calling to mind some arbitrary types of information such as the number of days in each month. You could still whip out your diary to find out the number of days in the present month, but I expect that you repeat to yourself:

Thirty days hath September,
April, June and November
And all the rest have thirty-one
Save for February alone.

Of course, if you forget the rhyme you are stuck. Someone said that his version went like this:

Thirty days hath September,
All the rest I can't remember!

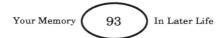

Another way of remembering the lengths of the months is to extend your clenched fists before you, knuckles uppermost, and then beginning with January on the knuckle of your left little finger, the 31-day months are all on the knuckles, with the shorter months on the dips between them.

Schoolteachers, although not going to the lengths of the Rev Brayshaw, frequently teach their pupils mnemonics to aid them in their studies. When they get tired of the children's bad spelling, they teach them:

I before E – Except after C

and:
StationERY – for a lettER,
StationARY – for the immobile porter, 'ARRY at the railway station.

Likewise in Geography there are first-letter mnemonics for the Great Lakes of Canada (H O M E S), and many other such features. I expect that you remember some of them from your childhood.

Victorian cooks, who were not always very literate, used to have a great store of kitchen mnemonics by which they taught their lore to their understudies, such as the relation between the tablespoon and the teaspoon as a measure – one big T equals three little ts. Mnemonics certainly have their place in daily living. When Daylight Saving was introduced in 1916, many people became muddled and altered their clocks the wrong way (and some still do) until some genius announced that it was easy:
Spring forward – fall back.

THE STORY METHOD
There is a further method which depends on making up a story that links up all the words to be remembered. Here we are backing up the other types of remembering with another kind that was discussed earlier – episodic memory, which is concerned with events that

happened in the past. Consider the following list:

MAN
WOOD
DEATH
NOBLE
BICYCLE
COAT
PORRIDGE
TRAVEL
OUT
FLOG
SNEERING
EARTH
SCARRED
KNEE
ROBUSTLY

This is a jumble of nouns, adjectives, prepositions and so forth, and so is especially difficult to remember. Could you learn such a list of words? You may say 'No, and I wouldn't want to!', but I must emphasise that this, as with other exercises, is not intended to have any practical value in itself. It is directed to demonstrate how the Story Method can be used to master even the most unpromising material. I have worked on this list and produced the following story, which links the words in the order they were given:

A MAN went into a WOOD where he met DEATH riding a NOBLE BICYCLE. The machine was noble because it had a COAT of arms on it. He asked Death if he wanted any PORRIDGE, for he was a TRAVEL(ling) salesman OUT to FLOG porridge. Death was SNEERING at his offer and threw EARTH at him. The earth was so hot it SCARRED his KNEE and made him shout ROBUSTLY.

The story is utter nonsense, yet if you force yourself to read nonsense, its very absurdity gives it a certain memorable quality, and if you read it through just once more and try to visualize what happened, then close the book, you will be able to reproduce much of this list of assorted words in the original order.

Reading a sensible story would not give the component words such a memorable quality. This illustrates a very interesting thing about memory: if you have ever looked at pictures that are known as 'surrealist', you will probably have experienced their peculiarly disturbing and memorable quality. Surrealist pictures bring together objects and settings that are not logically connected: a mermaid may be emerging from a grand piano, a frying pan may contain ornate jewellery, and a rather dirty pig may be lounging on a plush Victorian sofa in a drawing room which is unremarkable except that all the pictures are of detailed surgical operations. Some people find such surrealist art highly irritating and even offensive. They say that it is silly, grotesque, and an insult to conventional art. Yet they cannot easily forget these pictures.

What appears to happen is that when you look at a picture (or read a story) you want to make sense of it, and your mind will dwell on it until you have done so. You continue to work on it in some sense unconsciously, even when you want to forget about it. This technique is used by advertisers in trying to make their products memorable, hence the TV commercials that may be a little difficult to understand, and you have to work out their full meaning.

If you wish to convince yourself of this and are a glutton for work, write down about 15 words randomly selected from a dictionary, and then make up a story that in some way connects them, and you will find, perhaps to your surprise, that you will remember that list of words perhaps for weeks.

CHUNKING

This is a device that depends upon the capacity of the short-term memory to take in what is perceived (or heard) 'at a glance', to work on it and encode it in the long-term memory. A lot of experimental work has gone into investigating just how extensive this capacity is, and the answer that has emerged from most investigations is that it is limited to about seven items. Thus if you saw before you three printed letters, Q, F, M, you would have no difficulty in registering them in your short-term memory, and you could easily repeat them a minute or so later. Three items is well within the short-term memory's capacity. If you were presented with six letters all at once (or heard them read aloud) it is possible that you might make a mistake in repeating them for you would be approaching the capacity of your short-term memory. Anything over seven letters would certainly be risking a mistake in repetition.

Letters are individual items, and so are whole words. Thus you would have no difficulty in taking in and repeating a list of three like, CAT, BOTTLE, HAY. Again, if there were as many as six words in the list you would be approaching the limit of the capacity of your short-term memory.

Chunking is the technique of combining together several items to form a 'chunk', and thus a great deal of material can be held in the short-term memory, provided it is meaningfully related and does not much exceed seven chunks. Consider the following example: if you just glance at what is printed below, do you think that you could reproduce it accurately after a minute or two ?

FRSR
AFIT
VOBE
RIPU
SACI
DARP

The 24 letters on the previous page are grouped as six items of meaningless combinations, but they are not chunks that can be immediately registered. However, these letters can be arranged in eight chunks that are meaningful, and hence can be taken in and probably repeated accurately even though they exceed seven in number.

FRS   RIP
RAF   USA
ITV   CID
OBE   ARP

These three-letter combinations are probably quite familiar to you, so you recognize them at-a-glance and can register them as units.

With this information you can apply the technique of chunking in all sorts of situations, forewarned that you should limit your number of chunks to about seven. It is a very useful technique because you can adapt it to your own particular needs and capacities in material memorable to you. You can use it with imagery that is visual or auditory just as you please. If you are a history buff, you can convert a string of numbers such as 994848066789673 into historical dates simply by inserting the figure 1 and regular gaps, thus producing 1994 1848 1066 1789 1673. Chunking is a very useful technique for memorizing long and complicated telephone numbers.

One illustration of chunking that is frequently referred to is the capacity of chess-masters to look at the pieces on a chessboard where a game is in progress for a few seconds and then turn away, apparently having 'photographed' the position of all the pieces, a seemingly miraculous capacity. What the chess master has done is to represent quite a complex arrangement of pieces as a few chunks of meaningful inter-relationships between the pieces, and register them, just as you or I could remember if we saw letters and not pieces on the board, provided that the letters were arranged into meaningful words. If the pieces are placed randomly on the board so that they make no sense in terms of a game of chess, then the chess master is as little able to remember their position as you would be if you saw letters scattered randomly across the board.

Chunking would be a technique that could be applied to memorizing the shopping list that I presented earlier in this chapter. If you turn back to it you will see that the 10 items are written down in a random order as far as their practical significance goes, but they could be conveniently re-arranged into chunks according to their actual significance, thus:

Coffee-powder – tea – sugar – milk
Bread – butter – cake
Bleach – shoe polish – matches.

You would thus have three chunks to remember instead of 10 items. You have possibly been using the method of chunking for many years in some situations, without realizing how wide its applications are.

HOW OFTEN DO YOU USE MNEMONICS ?

The kinds of mnemonics that have been used have changed as society has become more complex and more dominated by technology. Whereas it used to be largely a matter of formalized rhymes, with the growth of writing and general education people have depended more and more on diaries and other written records. With the development of technology there have been inventions such as alarm clocks to remind us when to get up, and in the present age of sophisticated electronics all sorts of gadgets have been developed.

I was once complaining to a friend much younger than myself that I feared that my memory must be getting worse as I sometimes forgot important engagements. It was all very well to write them down in my diary, but how was I to remember to look at my diary at the proper time? He cheered me by saying that some of his colleagues in a university teaching department not only carried diaries in which they wrote, but diaries which were electronic and bleeped to remind them that they had to be consulted at appropriate times.

One researcher carried out a survey to determine how often people used mnemonic devices, and he compared a group of students, both male and female, with a group of women who were mainly house-wives. They were first interviewed fairly informally, and asked nine questions, and then given the list of memory aids which is reproduced below. You are not expected to read through this long list of memory aids – rather, I present it in its entirety so that you may dip into it when you feel inclined. If you are going to take seriously the matter of improving your memory by methods described in this book, you will probably want to devise your own mnemonic techniques, and here is a very comprehensive list offered so that you may choose to adapt some of them to your own purposes, according to what suits your individual preferences.

LIST OF MEMORY AIDS GIVEN TO THE SUBJECTS *
* Questions 1 – 9 were asked informally and are not given here.

10   Shopping lists.

11   First-letter 'memory aids'. For example the first letters of **Richard of York Gave Battle in Vain** give the colours of the rainbow.

12   Diary.

13   Rhymes. For example *In Fourteen hundred and ninety-two, Columbus sailed the ocean blue* aids memory of the date.

14   The place method (method used since classical times).
The items in a list to be remembered are imagined in a series of familiar locations. When recall is required, one 'looks' again in these familiar locations.

15   Writing on your hand what you need to remember.

16   The story method. For learning a list of items in order, a story is made up that connects them.

17   Mentally re-tracing a sequence of past events or actions in order to aid memory of something that happened, or to remember when you last had something you have now lost, and where you might have left it.

18   Alarm clock/radio (for waking up only).

19   Cooker timer with alarm or bell (for cooking purposes only).

20   Does your watch have an alarm system? (Yes / No).

21   Alarm clock/watch/radio/timer for purposes other than waking or cooking.
     • 21a Specify type(s) of apparatus used.
     • 21b Specify what you use the alarm to remind you of.

22   The peg method. Before this method can be used, the learner has to associate a word with each number up to, say, 50 – eg, 'one is a bun; two is a shoe; three is a tree . . .' Once this has been learned, lists of items may be remembered in the following way. The first is imagined or associated in some way with 'bun', the second with 'shoe' and so on.

23   Turning numbers into letters (eg, for telephone numbers).

24   Memos (eg, writing yourself special notes).
     • 24a Specify type of memo.

25 **Face-name association.** A mnemonic for learning peoples names is to change their names into something meaningful, and then look for an unusual feature of their faces and then to associate the two; eg, red-bearded Mr Hiles may be imagined with hills growing out of his beard.

26 **Alphabetical searching.** When trying to recall a name or word, one can go through the alphabet, letter by letter, to find the initial letter; eg, 'Does his name begin with A . . . , B . . . , Ah yes! C ! It's Clark.'

27 Calendar / year planner / wall chart.
  • 27a Specify how used.

28 Asking somebody else to remind you.

29 Leaving something in a special place so that it will be encountered at a time it needs to be remembered.

30 Other idiosyncratic external memory aids, eg, knotted handkerchief, changing rings to unfamiliar positions on fingers, turning wristwatch to underside of wrist.
  • 30a Specify aids used.

31 Other methods of committing things to memory
  • 31a Please describe these clearly.

32 Other methods of retrieving things from memory.
  • 32a Please describe these clearly.

Reproduced by permission of the author, Dr John E. Harris, and the Psychonomic Society Inc., from *Memory and Cognition* 1980, Vol. 8, (1).

The subjects were asked to rate each of the items on a six-point scale indicating how frequently they used these memory aids.

This investigation showed that everyone interviewed used some form of mnemonic devices, and these were mostly external aids rather than the psychological devices that have been described in this book. The most popular external aids were diaries, lists, calendars and timing devices. There were no striking differences between the students and the older group of women, and I am pretty sure that your use of memory aids would be much according to this pattern. Again I would emphasise that I am not trying to teach you a bag of tricks, and passing this off as 'improving your memory', as do so many commercial memory courses and paperback memory books. The sole purpose of this chapter is to increase your understanding of how your memory works, and leave it to you how, in the light of your increased knowledge, to tackle the problems of learning and memory that you encounter.

APPENDIX TO CHAPTER 5
For how many of these Japanese words can you give the meaning? They are from **List A** and **List B** on pages 89 and 90 given here in mixed order.

1	KOFU	11	DADDAKO
2	GOGO	12	KIROKU
3	FUKUMU	13	NEGIRU
4	DOJO	14	KOSHO
5	SENKO	15	OHAYO
6	RODOSHA	16	WAKARU
7	WARUI	17	SHOTAI
8	SHAKO	18	KOFUKU
9	NEKO	19	ONNA
10	UKETORI	20	NISEMONO

6

IMPROVING YOUR MEMORY

In order to devise schemes for improving memory, it is first necessary to measure how good your memory is so you'll be able to measure your improvement.

MEASURING RECALL

If you were to learn a reasonably long poem at one sitting so that you could recall it perfectly on one final trial, on re-testing your recall next day it is likely that you would make one or two errors, and if you were tested in a week's time (without having had the opportunity to rehearse the poem) you would probably make a larger number of errors. Re-testing after a month (again with no rehearsal) would result in still more errors. These errors would occur because of the feeding into your memory-bank of all sorts of ongoing information that would distort and cancel out some of the knowledge of the poem by the various mechanisms described earlier. It would, of course, be possible to learn the poem word perfect so that you would never make an errors in repeating it, but that would require considerable over-learning, and not just learning to the criterion of one perfect repetition.

Measuring the memory of each of a group of individuals by the method of free recall may be achieved by reading aloud a story to them, and then after a lapse of time, asking each one to write what he or she remembers of the story, Their reproductions may then be marked for accuracy and coverage of all the salient points. It is interesting that this method reveals not only that people vary very much in to their capacity for recall, but the content of the story will determine to a considerable degree, how memorable it is to them. An extreme example of this was shown by one psychologist who read to his students a story entitled *The War of the Ghosts* which he had culled from the folklore of a tribe of Canadian Indians. It was astonishing how little the students could remember of this story, for to Western ears it was utterly bizarre, and hence lacking in a form that could be easily comprehended and assimilated. I have tried this experiment myself using this story, and when the members of the group each read aloud their remembered versions of it, it seemed as though some people had listened to an entirely different story!

But leaving aside cultural variations, in any group of people there will be considerable differences in general interests, and this affects powers of recall. Thus a sailor may recall in considerable detail one of Conrad's nautical stories, a horsey countryman one of Surtees' Jorrocks stories, and a 'man of action' (in reality or fantasy) may best remember some of Hemingway's stories.

Stories and poems are, of course, meaningful material, and the rhyming line-endings make the latter easier to memorize. A test of memory may also be carried out by getting the subject to learn a long list of words until he can repeat it perfectly on the final trial. Memory for the list will likewise show a decrement with time, unless periodically rehearsed.

Another method is to get the subject to learn what is known as a 'paired associate' list, such as: corkscrew - cow,   seaside - paper, timber - faith,   cooking - loneliness, etc, there being no logical con-nection between the words in each pair. Memory can be tested by giving the first word and asking the subject to say its pair.

Serial learning is something different; it requires the subject not only to be able to recall a list of words, but to repeat them in the order in which they were presented. To some extent this is like paired associate learning, because each word suggests the one that follows it.

Measurement by recognition. It is easier to recognize whether you do or do not remember something, than to recall it unprompted. You have huge stores of facts in your memory that you cannot call to mind

by an effort of will, but if they are presented to you, there is a greater chance of your recognizing them as being part of your store of knowledge. Thus if I present you with the following questions as a free recall task, I wonder how many you can answer.

What is the meaning of?

Amulet
Querulous
Temerity
Fecund
Abnegate

Even if you knew the meaning, did it take you a minute or two to remember it? But if I present the words as follows, I think that the meaning will come to you more quickly.

Identify the correct meaning:
Amulet: arm-band, brooch, marker, charm, weapon, lock
Querulous: peaceful, peevish, tired, empty, kind, interested
Temerity: wisdom, cowardice, rashness, humour, luck, baseness
Fecund: barren, weary, honourable, thin, fertile, thin
Abnegate: aspire, renounce, claim, distinguish, rebel, ridicule

Words are, of course, templates in the brain, and it is easier to get the appropriate word when you simply scan the six templates that are provided for each word in the list above. The power of recognition that the brain has is truly amazing, and this is especially true of faces. How the template of a face, picture, word, sound or feeling is formed is a real mystery, but you use these templates all the time in daily living. One interesting fact is that while younger people are better at free recall, powers of recognition do not decline with age, although older people may take a little longer to respond, because they have such a large number of templates to scan.

The method of savings. Suppose you tell me that you believe that you learned something at school – say the names of the chemical elements – but you have absolutely no memory of them now. If, however, you tried to re-learn the list, and I compared your performance with that of some people who knew that they had never studied chemistry at school, or had any contact with it in adult life, I am sure that you would learn the list much quicker than the others. The 'savings' would be due to your hidden memory.

An example of proof of memory by the savings method was reported by one psychologist who experimented with his own son's memory. When the boy was only as young as 15 months he started reading passages of Greek to him, and continued this until he was three years old. Of course the Greek meant very little to him, but his father reckoned that some of it would be memorized. At the age of eight he got the boy to learn various passages of Greek, some of which were the original pieces he had read to him when he was very young, and on these there was an indication that he learned them more quickly than the new passages. He repeated the experiment when his son was 14 and again at 18 with the same results, although the percentage of time saved, comparing the learned with the unlearned passages, decreased as he grew older. The time it takes to re-learn something is reduced if, although it is apparently 'forgotten', it is significantly lodged in your long-term memory.

IMPROVEMENT IN THE LABORATORY AND IN DAILY LIFE
Most of the first attempts at teaching people to improve their memories took place in psychological laboratories where they were taught various skills, many of them being the mnemonic methods.

They were given tasks like learning lists of words, and even lists of 'nonsense syllables' like KUK, WIC, JIR, and the learned the best way to learn paired-associate words, memorize strings of digits, etc, etc. By testing them before the course and then some time after it, it was evident that the participants did indeed improve their memory skills as measured by laboratory tests. But some of them complained that they still had as much difficulty in everyday life due to their faulty memories. This criticism was met by psychologists who claimed that some of the problems were more imaginary than real, and they pointed out that many older people, particularly if they were depressed, or influenced by the negative stereotypes of ageing that are current, would blame their memories for all sorts of dissatisfactions with life. There is certainly some justice in this answer to the criticisms, and the remedy for these peoples' troubles do not lie in giving them memory training, but in advising them how to improve their way of life, a matter that is by no means easy.

However, although there is some evidence that improvement in the laboratory does predict improvement in the memory problems of everyday life, the effect is not very strong, and psychologists have sought to make their memory training programmes more relevant to people's everyday needs, as will be described later in this chapter.

PRACTICAL APPLICATIONS TO MEMORY TRAINING

Initial measurement by self-rating. Psychologists have applied these various ways of measuring memory, to the improvement of courses designed to teach people how to develop a better memory. Earlier, a newspaper article was referred to about a tennis champion who thought he was improving his powers of memory by exercises based on physical work-outs to build up muscle power. I pointed out that as no measures of improvement were used, there was really no evidence that the exercises did any good at all. In properly conducted courses for teaching memory skills, the participants' general memory ability is measured before the beginning of the course, and then again, probably some months later, after the benefits of the course will have time to take effect. By this means the value of the course can be assessed.

A memory questionnaire. Below is a questionnaire that is based on various inquiries into memory, and closely resembles one that was used before and after a training course in memory in which 34 men and women between the ages of 52 and 81 participated

MEMORY QUESTIONNAIRE

Here are questions about common forgetfulness. Please indicate how often you have problems in each particular area by putting a tick in the appropriate column.

	NEVER	RARELY	OCCASIONALLY	OFTEN
A You forget the names of people you have just met ?	☐	☐	☐	☐
B You forget to keep appointments, even those written in your diary ?	☐	☐	☐	☐
C You forget routine things like watering plants and taking medicine ?	☐	☐	☐	☐
D You get lost in new places or where you have seldom visited ?	☐	☐	☐	☐
E You forget where you have put things like glasses, handbag or wallet ?	☐	☐	☐	☐
F When reading, you forget what you've just read and have to go back and re-read it ?	☐	☐	☐	☐
G You start saying something, then forget what you wanted to say ?	☐	☐	☐	☐
H You have trouble in learning new things, like card games or typing ?	☐	☐	☐	☐
I When you've several things to do, you forget to do one or more of them ?	☐	☐	☐	☐
J You forget names of common objects, have trouble finding words you want ?	☐	☐	☐	☐

This questionnaire is based on researches by various people, but especially by Cathy M McEvoy and James R Moon, of the University of South Florida, and published in *Practical aspects of Memory: Current Research and Issues*. (Eds M M Gruneberg, P E Morris & R N Sykes. Chichester: John Wiley & Sons, to whom acknowledgement is given.)

If you would like to see how your memory for everyday things compares with that of a group of 40 people over the age of 60 whom I tested, do the following:

Take a blank sheet of paper and write the letters A to J in a vertical column. Then put your rating against each item, according to how often you experience the problem. The responses of the group I tested were as follows:

	NEVER	RARELY	OCCASIONALLY	OFTEN
A You forget the names of people you have just met ?	0	4	23	13
B You forget to keep appointments, even those written in your diary ?	24	11	5	0
C You forget routine things like watering plants and taking medicine ?	13	15	11	1
D You get lost in new places or where you have seldom visited ?	16	15	6	3
E You forget where you have put things like glasses, handbag or wallet ?	4	7	19	10
F When reading, you forget what you've just read and have to go back and re-read it ?	3	9	25	3
G You start saying something, then forget what you wanted to say ?	8	9	20	3
H You have trouble in learning new things, like card games or typing ?	12	17	9	2
I When you've several things to do, you forget to do one or more of them ?	5	14	19	2
J You forget names of common objects, have trouble finding words you want ?	3	9	18	10

The responses you gave are not necessarily related to your age. As one person pointed out, she had always had very great difficulty in learning anything like new card games.

A PRACTICAL TRAINING COURSE

A questionnaire very similar to the one given above was used to measure the memory of a group of people with an average age of 68 years. As you can see the questionnaire refers to ten different areas of difficulty in everyday life, and each one was tackled individually in the workshops as follows:

Names and faces (A). The participants learned to apply the imagery mnemonics which have been described in Chapter 5 (remember imagining 'hill' sprouting from the beard of Mr Hiles ?) and also they were taught how to associate a new name to someone already known. Thus if Mr Wells was noticeably short and fat, and you had once known Charlie Wells who was tall and scraggy, then the contrast between the two men would be a link of association. In learning names it was also stressed that you should try to repeat a new person's name in conversation with them soon after meeting them. Another technique for remembering names is to rehearse the names of people whom you do not meet often when you know that you are going to meet them again. In this training course, the fact that these people were meeting together periodically provided an excellent opportunity to practise these name-learning techniques.

Appointments (B). Here about the best thing to do in remembering appointments that are not routine, is to use external aids such as diaries, marked calendars, and even old-fashioned tricks of tying a knot in your handkerchief, wearing your watch on the wrong wrist, and even sticking a tiny label on the face of your watch. 'What on earth does this knot in my handkerchief mean ? Ah, I must look at my diary!'

Routine tasks (C). Perhaps you forget to carry out routine tasks such as reminding your husband or wife to take medicine every four hours (you know that it will be forgotten unless you say something). There are other things that can be linked to events that happen regularly. When your spouse turns on the six o'clock news every evening, you are reminded to water the houseplants. At weekends when the news is not at six o'clock, you have to fix on some other regular event to remind you of this chore.

Spatial orientation (D). Learning to get around effectively in the environment bothers some people a lot, and on this course they were taught that they should not leave it to chance, but make a systematic effort to use both verbal cues (the shoe shop is next to Boots the chemist – how convenient!) and visual codes (the Alliance building looks as though it was staring at the Catholic Church). Again, when you go down a totally new street, do not just look at the landmarks as you pass them, but keep turning round to note how the street and its landmarks look when you will be coming down it from the opposite direction. Some people hate using maps, but there is really no difficulty if you set yourself the task of patiently trying to relate maps to the environment, and not being too shy to ask people to help you to learn skills at the age of 65 that you should have learned at 10.

Locating objects (E). Many people have difficulty in locating objects in their homes because they never take the trouble to organize where they put them. With some thought you can plan just where objects are to be stored in places which are related to their function. Thus the box of plasters should obviously be placed in the medicine cupboard in the bathroom, but it is a good idea to have a second box in the kitchen cupboard by the stove where they are readily available when you burn yourself, or when the knife slips while you are chopping vegetables. And the car keys? That is up to you, but you should always put them in the same place. Just think of how objects should be – ideally – stored in the proper pigeon-holes of your memory-bank, and let your house be equally well organized.

Concentration (F). The participants in the course had stories read to them, shown on video, and read them for themselves, with the object of practising concentration. They tried to review the stories as they were presented, and relate them to what they already knew about the plots. They were encouraged to try to predict the events that they expected to take place in the unfolding of the stories.

THE RESULTS
Only the first six of the areas of concern, A – F on the questionairre, were the subject of the experience in the workshops; the other areas, G – J were not mentioned. This was deliberate, for it was intended to compare progress in the areas that were tackled with any changes that took place in the areas that were not mentioned, as only thus could it be determined whether the course was of any use. After the course was over, the participants were again given the original questionnaire and their original scores on each item were compared with their later scores. The results were moderately encouraging; for there was a definite improvement on items A, B, C and D, but not on the other items. The one disappointing item was item F which concerns concentration, on which there was no improvement. It was noted that on item D there was only slight improvement. The fact that there was no improvement on the four items that were not included in the workshop studies, is, of course, encouraging, because it indicates that the improvement in the other areas was not just due to the passage of time.

This study is important for it shows that you can improve your memory in the matters of everyday living, and that it is not just for tackling the tests that psychologists have devised in their laboratories. It must be stressed that such improvement involves hard work on the part of those who want to benefit, for there is no easy 'key to success' as some of the memory books imply. It is firstly a matter of understanding what you are trying to do, and then having understood what the problems are, to apply the methods that best suit you personally, and this involves getting to know yourself better. Are you predominantly a verbal type or a visual type ? Have you a good ear for what you hear, or would you much rather read about things than be told them? Are you fairly self-confident and optimistic, or are you rather prone to doubting your own abilities ? The following account of how a class of older people learned a poem illustrates these differences between individuals.

LEARNING A POEM

A group of people over the age of 60 were attending a course of seminars I was running devoted to 'Learning and memory in later life'. One of the exercises involved learning a poem by a special method. No. 1 of the group was given the poem printed in full, and she read it aloud; on her left was No. 2 who was given the printed poem but with some of the words left blank, and she tried to read it by filling in the gaps with her memory of what she had just heard. On her left was No. 3 whose copy of the poem had even more gaps, and she also tried to read the poem in its entirety, and so it went on. As we went round the group, members had thinner and thinner versions of the poem, and the last person had a blank sheet from which she tried to 'read' it! It required two or three trials round the group before anyone could repeat the poem word-perfect, and it became apparent that some individuals were learning it much faster than others, and their advantage did not appear to relate to their position in the group. Obviously, what learning depends on under these conditions is a good auditory memory, since the poem (mistakes and all) is constantly being read aloud.

Members were then given a full version of the poem to take home and learn, and when the group next met, everyone was asked to write it out from memory. Naturally, the more diligent individuals could produce better versions of the poem, but in the lengthy discussion about learning that followed it became apparent that diligence was not the only factor involved. Some members complained that they had tried really hard to learn it but could produce very little, whereas others expressed surprise that anyone should find difficulty in learning such simple verses. I then introduced the group to a method of learning verse (or prose for that matter) by employing visual imagery and telling the story, as it were, by a series of imagined cartoons. This is, after all, what is done in the traditional strip cartoon. The poem which was studied has five verses and is by Dorothy Parker. For the sake of brevity I will give you only the first two:

THE WHISTLING GIRL

Back of my back, they talk of me,
Gabble and honk and hiss;
Let them batten, let them be –
Me, I can sing them this:

'Better to shiver beneath the stars,
Head on a faithless breast,
Than peer at night through rusted bars,
And share an irksome rest.

I then tried to illustrate it on the blackboard in the form of a strip cartoon, verse by verse, pointing out that there were some obvious visual images that could be conjured up, and invited each of them to have a go however little artistic skill they possessed. Perhaps something like this . . .

The effort of trying to tell a narrative in the form of pictures has the effect of anchoring it very firmly in the memory, and the person who said that she had had the greatest difficulty in trying to learn the poem produced a most amusing strip cartoon illustrating all that went on. She is a talented amateur artist and an illustrator of children's books, and she was delighted to discover a method of remembering verbal material in a way that was new to her. But not everyone was so struck with this method, particularly those who could learn and remember verbal material very easily.

WHAT KIND OF BAD MEMORY HAVE YOU ?
It is not very meaningful to say that you have a bad memory unless you say what you have a bad memory for. The result of a question-naire, like that shown a few pages back, demonstrates just how varied problems with memory are. Some may have great difficulty with C, E, and H, but little trouble with B and J, while the pattern of others' forgetfulness may be quite the reverse. These great differences between people partly depend upon the sort of lives they habitually lead. Thus someone living in a quiet village may meet very few new people and hence is seldom troubled by the problem of forgetting the names of those they have just met, whereas if you lead a busy social life it will seriously concern you to learn people's names. Nevertheless, although there is a good deal of specificity in the problems that you mostly encounter, an understanding of the under-lying mechanisms of memory will go a long way to enabling you to tackle any particular problem.

Again, you must ask yourself, have I really got a bad memory – is it worse now than it used to be ? In the days when you led much the same routine of life year after year you were not specially troubled by problems relating to memory, but now that you are, perhaps, living a very different sort of life after retirement, you may be faced with all sorts of new challenges and you become very con-scious of any lapses of memory. You may fear that you are becoming inadequate to cope with all the problems that beset you. Many people imagine that being retired means being put out to grass quietly, with no more hassle, but often the reverse is true. The prospect, if not the reality, of failing health and coming economic stringency may be a daunting one for many people.

A NEW LOOK AT MEMORY TRAINING

In the last few decades there has been a good deal of research into memory training in three areas: the rehabilitation of people who have suffered head injuries, including strokes and mechanical violence, the improvement of the abilities of university students who need to study a great deal, the improvement of memory in older people. It has become apparent that different methods are appropriate to these three areas. In this book I am concerned with the last-named area. What might be called the 'traditional methods' of memory training have come under increasing criticism, and progress has been made in modifying them to achieve a greater rate of success with different groups.

Traditional methods date back to the ancient Greeks and the story of the poet Simonides has already been mentioned as the alleged inventor of the 'place method' for remembering the different points to be tackled in proper order in an orators speech. But Simonides was solely concerned with the problems of orators. He was not concerned with such matters as remembering to keep a dental appointment, or whether he remembered to feed the cat before going out.

The traditional methods most often advised in memory books and in commercially run courses, include many of the gimmicks described in Chapter 5. All of these methods have been found effective in improving memory for specific tasks immediately after they have been applied, and this has encouraged those who employed them in such training courses to believe in their efficacy as a general means of improving memory on a permanent basis.

THE RESULTS OF RESEARCH

In general, traditional methods have been perfected in psychological laboratories, and it has been found that, with training, people can

show dramatic improvement in such abilities as remembering long lists of words, or strings of numbers, and remembering the capital cities of every country in the world. The ability does not last very long, however, neither does it generalize to other areas of memorizing – such as keeping dental appointments and feeding the cat. In the study discussed above, on which the questionnaire given earlier was based, it was shown that the participants' memory for everyday things (problem areas A,B,C, and D) could definitely be improved with appropriate training, but this improvement did not generalize to the areas which had not been specially studied. If we turn to the area of physical skills, the analogy will make the matter plainer.

Training in the physical skill of playing tennis will not improve ability in long-distance running, and training in running will not improve ability in playing ice hockey. Granted that ability in all these three athletic sports demand adequate motivation, proper diet, adequate rest, and good muscular tone, but so does the ability in 'remembering' demand adequate motivation, reasonable physical health and proper current nutrition.

Thus in the area of physical ability we take it for granted that skills will be quite specific, but as far as mental ability goes, people tend to cling to the idea that there is something called 'memory' that can be improved by some sort of magic. The reality is more mundane – provided that you have sufficient motivation, reasonable health and a proper understanding of how mental processes work you can greatly improve your efficiency in all sorts of areas of life where you have problems of 'forgetting'. And improving your efficiency means that you will have matters more under your control, and lead a happier and more interesting life.

Modern psychologists concerned with memory training have now come round to the approach that emphasises task-specific instruction, that is, if the task is learning how to recognize people you have just met and remember their names, the mechanisms involved are thoroughly explained and discussed and there will be intensive practice. If the problem is overcoming the tip-of-the-tongue blockage, similarly there will be full explanation and discussion followed by practical exercises. All this involves a reasonable amount of work by those concerned if the improvement is to be permanent.

Further, underlying improvement in every aspect of learning and memory, is the debunking of the many myths about memory such as those discussed earlier in this book. Otherwise, belief in these myths tends to rob you of your self-confidence and make you feel inadequate by virtue of age, and you expect not to perform intellectually as well as you ever did, although you must understand that you will function differently.

Equipped with adequate external aids, including spectacles for weak eyesight, hearing aids, walking sticks, false teeth, diaries, alarm clocks etc, and internal aids such as mnemonic techniques and a proper understanding of what is right for you personally, the world may be faced with confidence in your Third Age. What ? Do you reject all these external aids as being 'unnatural' ? You would surely not throw away your spectacles because they aren't 'natural' and declare that you are a poor old thing so other people must look after you ? The choice is yours.

7

WILL YOU CONTINUE TO MAKE PROGRESS ALL YOUR LIFE ?

MEMORY AT DIFFERENT STAGES OF LIFE

It should be apparent to you by now that in later life you are likely to have a somewhat over-stocked memory-bank of considerable complexity because you have been loading in memories for many years, and not always organizing your experiences in an orderly manner. It follows, therefore, that you have to work a good deal on the contents of your short-term memory in order that it will be anchored firmly in the memory-bank of the long-term memory. The young child with a relatively simple and uncluttered memory-bank has no such problem. Consider the example of a boy placed in a foreign school where the language is strange to him. Very soon he will begin to pick up the language, simply by playing with children who speak it. He does not need to work specially hard to learn the new language; he acquires it much as he learnt his mother tongue in infancy.

An interesting example of this is related by the novelist Anthony Burgess, who went to live in Malta with his little son. Burgess was somewhat proud of his ability to learn foreign languages, so he set to work with a dictionary, phrase book and Maltese grammar, supplemented by conversation with the natives of the island, to learn the language. Later he was surprised and somewhat envious to find that his little boy could speak more Maltese than he could, and prattled fluently with the children of the neighbourhood. Naturally, as Burgess was an adult, he eventually learned to speak the language more correctly, and to have a wider vocabulary than his son, but he found the learning of this difficult language effortful, in contrast with the child who had acquired it without having to work at it.

You probably found it easier to learn new things, and to

remember them better, when your memory-bank was less fully stocked, and simpler than it is today. Comparing the older brain with the younger, there are advantages for each. Now you are older you may have a greater understanding of many things. I do not mean things like bookkeeping, which you may have practised in your youth but have not done for 40 years, but a greater grasp of those things that interest you and give you satisfaction in life. Because of your richer stock of knowledge, you now have a greater maturity of judgement, and a greater appreciation of various things that you did not enjoy fully when first encountered years ago.

For example, in my later years I have re-read a number of books that I encountered in middle age, and regarded as being of no great interest. On second reading, I was surprised to find what fascinating books they were now that I had the background knowledge to appreciate them fully. This experience is reported by many of my acquaintances in the Third Age. However, I am as aware as everyone else in my age group of the disadvantages of later life; you have to work harder at things that would have been learned with much less effort in your younger years. When I refer to the fact that the memory-bank of the older person is somewhat over-stocked, I do not imply that the brain is of limited capacity, in the same way as a computer might approach the limit of its storage capacity. The situation is quite different. The capacity of the brain is so large that we never approach its limit. But inevitably some of the material in your memory-bank is less than well organized, and it cannot be easily retrieved. Not only is there difficulty in retrieving some of the material but some memories actually distort and inhibit others.

So what do you do ? Are you so intimidated by the difficulties to be encountered in later life that you are prepared to give up the struggle to retain an efficient working intellect, or will you take up the challenge and continue to make progress for the whole of your life ? It may sound a bit of a tall order to suggest that you should make 'progress', for you may feel that you have to run hard in order to stand still ! But I do mean progress. You have a lifetime of experience no matter what your occupation and your education have been, and you can build on that. Potentially, you are now a more effective person than you ever have been. Of course, if you have been an athlete you can no longer depend upon your athleticism to be a source of satisfaction in later life, although your knowledge and expertise in the whole subject may be. We all have the same experience. Our minds become richer as we go through life while our physical powers weaken, and although medical science has done wonders during the present century to combat the ills of the flesh and to give us a longer life-expectancy, one day we are all going to fall off our perches, and it is to be hoped that this will occur in the midst of rewarding and worthwhile activity.

THE ENEMIES OF PROGRESS
Before entering the fray, determined that the years of your Third Age shall be as meaningful and enjoyable as any of the other ages you have been through, it is wise to consider just what you are up against. The obstacles come both from without and within. Unless you have had a very unusual life experience, you will have inherited the usual expectancy that when you are 'old':
you have to accept the fact that you are 'past it' in every way. You are now an oldie, a wrinkly, a has-been. You are a bit weak in the head and cannot be expected to carry out a proper job because you would make a mess of it, and that is why they retired you at the appropriate age. You may have some value as a child-minder to your grand-children in order to free your middle-aged children to get on with their lives (which are important in contrast with yours), and all your concerns must take second place when this is required of you. If you have money it is not really yours to spend, for it must be conserved for your inheritors. If you are rendered single, you must be resigned to stay that way because it would be bizarre, ridiculous, to find a new partner, and anyway, who would want you at your age? Of course you forget things; of course you cannot be expected to learn anything new,

for you are old. You had better retire from life, accept your limitations, and quietly wait for your death.

The above is an exaggeration, and you have certainly never heard it put so crudely. However, such a statement is not so very far from the stereotype of 'the old' that is conveyed by society, and in youth you may have had opinions and feelings about ageing and the aged rather like the above. In later life it is natural to have strong misgivings about your own abilities because of your previous expectations, and you are likely seriously to underrate your capacity for further development. On top of everything else, you have probably less physical energy, and you may have health problems to cope with. Consequently you may feel that it would be far simpler just to retire into a metaphorical chimney corner and accept your growing limitations.

Perhaps you had hoped that in this book some 'secret' of memory whereby you would be able, if not to eliminate, at least greatly to palliate the difficulties that you are encountering would be revealed. In my experience in running courses for the improvement of memory, a frequent question at the beginning is 'What is the secret of acquiring a reliable memory?' People expect a simple answer – that I will tell them the secret of a good memory – and some are disappointed to learn that there is no such secret, and no one method of improving their powers. To improve memory, even for the most mundane things in daily living, you have to work at whatever problems you encounter – and continue to work at them in the ways that have been discussed in this book.

SHOULD YOU MAKE EVEN GREATER EFFORTS?

Try not only to overcome your present problems, but to aspire to progress and acquire greater abilities, greater skills in whatever interests you have and for which you have potential talents. 'What', you may reply, 'me, in spite of my stiff joints, failing eyesight, double hernia, partial deafness, bad digestion and a tendency to gout?' To which I reply, 'No, not in spite of but because of your stiff joints, etc!' You will never be a demon on the squash court again, so the time has come for you to develop your other talents. Regarding your memory, it is as though you were the sole Director of a corporation that is now large and continually growing, and you can never retire from this position. In the library analogy of memory outlined earlier, I pointed out that a public library is not a limited collection of books, because new books are coming in the whole time, and have to be catalogued and shelved. Many overworked librarians may say, 'Oh, I wish that they would stop publishing more and more books and swelling our collection!' That is what is happening to your memory-bank, and will continue to happen for the rest of your life, for memory is not a static bank of knowledge; it is being edited the whole time, and forgetting is part of the dynamic process over which you must maintain your control.

In discussing the acquisition of a foreign language, I contrasted the mind of a child with that of an adult, and pointed out that each of the stages of life had its problems and its advantages. So the mind of a middle-aged adult may be compared with that of someone in the Third Age. The adult cannot passively absorb some sorts of knowledge, like that of a foreign language that is spoken all around, as the child does, but the child has to work hard in school because the task is not just the absorbing of facts, but the building up of the structure and the methods by which all facts can be learned and retained. The adult has the advantage that the structure has already been formed, and although she or he may believe that they have forgotten practically all that they learned in school, if it were really necessary they could rapidly re-learn any subject that they have studied at school.

ENTERING THE THIRD AGE

So it is in the Third Age. In later life, according to your past
experience, you have a huge range of potentialities within your
memory-bank – unfulfilled aspirations, half-developed talents, latent
skills that you have forgotten about. After retirement you have the
marvellous opportunity to exercise a wide range of choices – choice of
what to revive, to continue, to develop. Memory for a particular
group of interests can be revived, old skills rapidly re-learnt.
Although you may experience the constraints of an economic pinch,
and of physical ills, it is in some ways like the end of adolescence with
the opening up of a new phase of life before you. Either you can
approach it timorously, with the depressing and derogatory stereotype of 'old age' before you, or you can approach it expansively, with a
determination to enjoy your Third Age to the full.

Retirement can be a bore, and it is reported that the period of
approaching it is sometimes a time of anxiety, but as one team of
investigators reported, 'We found that retirement is for many husbands
and wives a mere bugaboo – distressing in anticipation, but enjoyable
after it occurs'. The enjoyment of retirement depends upon a number of
things, and has different implications for men and women.

However much men may grumble about the stress of daily work, most of their friends are associated with their employment, and most of their leisure habits are conditioned by their weekly working routine. Unless they can look beyond this pattern of the working world, retirement may become a deprivation, hence the founding of the Pre-retirement Association and the development of pre-retirement courses. If his wife is not working outside the home, a man may get in her way when he retires, and if she is in a job supplementing a meagre family income, he may find himself being pressurized into household chores to which he is unaccustomed, and rather resents.

In times past, many older women were in reality, holding down two jobs, the paid employment and being a housewife. There is no retirement from the latter job, so women did not have the same problems as men. The present generation of women retiring are likely to have worked, so retirement is for them more of a positive experience. She continues to run the household but is relieved of the strain of working at two jobs

ARE YOU A TASK-ORIENTED TYPE OR A LOTOS-EATER ?

In writing this book I have generally addressed the reader directly as 'you', but there is a disadvantage to this approach. The majority of readers will be people in later life, and all researchers who have studied the process of ageing are agreed on one thing: older individuals differ from one another rather more than do younger adults. The more people age the more they develop individuality, so who is this hypothetical 'you', and what are her or his characteristics ? Are you a 'task-oriented' person who loves to buzz around organizing things, sitting on committees, and setting the world to rights ? Or are you the opposite, a lotos-eater who prefers to lie in the sun, who spends hours and hours just reading novels, listening to music and chatting with friends ? These two types of individuals will adjust to retirement in different ways, but either may be equally fulfilled providing that they adopt a life-style that suits them. They will be ill-advised if they try to follow one particular course of action because it is recommended by a 'specialist'.

The true lotos-eater probably doesn't need this book but, as has been said before, the best way of becoming an 'old dog' is to refrain from learning any new tricks as longevity is generally associated with a very active life. But this does not hold to the same degree for everyone. In any case, most people would agree that it is the quality rather than the length of life that they value. Like those in the Odyssey they turn away from the hurly-burly of the world and say, as Tennyson relates in his poem:

Let us swear an oath, and keep it with an equal mind,
In the hollow Lotos-land to live and lie reclined
On the hills and live like gods together, careless of mankind.
For they lie beside their nectar . . .

MIND-STRETCHERS IN LATER LIFE

Concern about the memory and learning abilities of healthy people in later life is a comparatively recent thing; it has been described as a modern 'growth industry'. Up to about 20 years ago it was generally accepted that the abilities of normal people would naturally deteriorate around the years of retirement, and professional concern was directed to the small minority of older people who develop diseases and traumatic injury which lead to metal degeneration. Various factors are responsible for the present concern with the memory of normal elderly people which really began in the 1970s. One of the precipitating causes was the social concern of the generation that was then coming to the age of retirement. They were the generation who were young adults in the immediate post-war years, and had been concerned with such social changes as the founding of the Welfare State, the growth of a militant feminist movement, and the radical changes in outlook towards sexuality that began in the 1960s. You are probably actively concerned about your own memory now because of these social movements, whereas your parents would have

taken for granted any changes they noted in themselves.

Movements such as that of the 'Consultation of Older and Younger Adults' (commonly referred to as the Gray Panthers) began in the USA, in the 1970s, and it is worth quoting the manifesto of their founder, Maggie Kuhn:

We did not select our name, the name selected us.
It describes who we are:

(i) We are older persons in retirement.

(ii) We are aware of the revolutionary nature of our time.

(iii) Although we differ with the strategy and tactics of some militant groups in our society, we share with them many of the goals of human dignity, freedom and self-development

(iv) We have a sense of humour. Our purpose is to celebrate the bonus years of retirement as a time for contributions to the new age of liberation and self-determination.

It is now quite unremarkable for retired people of any age to study for a degree at the Open University, such as a man who had left school at the age of 14, and had worked as a miner at the coal face for many years, who took early retirement at the age of 62 in order to get a local authority educational grant to work towards a degree at a red-brick university. He told me that he works the whole time with a dictionary at his elbow, and his writing is painfully slow, but he persists, and from what I have seen of his work, he has developed a fine clear style.

University studies are not to everyone's liking, and the common prejudice against the term 'university' has deterred some people from joining in the activities of one of the most remarkable organizations of our age, the University of the Third Age. This movement started in

France in 1972 where it was indeed associated with the French universities, but where it has spread to other countries, including Britain, it has taken different forms not necessarily connected with universities. The Universities of the Third Age (commonly referred to as U3As in the UK) are for retired people, although there is no lower age-limit for joining. They are entirely self-governing and self-financing, although in some cases small grants have been given by public and commercial bodies or charitable foundations. No educational qualifications are required for admission, no examinations conducted and no degrees or diplomas awarded. The great bulk of the teaching is carried out unpaid by members themselves, study groups often meeting in the members' homes or in rented accommodation. The topics studied include a very wide range of interests, such as foreign languages, literature, drama, history, classical and jazz music, archaeology, personal finance, and 'studies' merge into 'activities' such as bridge, chess, bird-watching, attending concerts and plays, and foreign travel. In fact, any interest that a member has can be developed by recruiting like-minded people to participate.

WILL IT BE LIKE BEING BACK IN THE GUIDES / SCOUTS AGAIN ?
Some people may be deterred by the word 'university' but many U3A activities are not at all academic in the usually accepted meaning of the word. You would not be 'examined' or shown to be wanting in comparison with your contemporaries. There may remain the feeling, however, that it might be like being back in the guides or scouts again, with task-oriented leaders jollying you along to be bright and active, when all you want to do is to hide in the bracken, munch sweets and read a magazine. Is there, in fact, any place for lotos-eaters in the U3A ?

One of the local U3As recently carried out a survey of its membership in order to find out more about their characteristics and to canvass their opinions about future development. One of the things that interested the management committee was what determined whether members would volunteer to act as tutors or class conveners, and propose subjects for study and activity. As the organization is based entirely on self-help and individual initiative, the programme of classes and activities depends on sufficient members being willing to originate ideas and put them into practice. In the survey questionnaire, which was completed anonymously, the following question was asked: 'Please indicate the sorts of reason that deter you from running a class or activity.' The answers were, of course, very varied, but they could be broken down into several groups.

One group simply gave their age as the reason: 'Age', 'I shall be 80 next August.'; 'Laziness (but I am 86)'; 'Unqualified and too old'; 'Too old! Other commitments'; 'Age – 82!'; 'Too old'. This excuse is highly revealing, and indicates the common idea that age in itself disqualifies (or excuses one) from taking initiative. It should be noted that some of these respondents may have been attending classes and activities provided by people older than themselves. A group of answers that will evoke special sympathy came from people who have been teachers of one sort and another and reply like this: 'I have been a teacher all my career, and now I want to learn and enjoy it, rather than preparing material and teaching others'; 'Having spent many years working and caring for others, I feel at my age, perhaps selfishly, I want to sit back'; 'I have spent my life as a teacher and I look forward to and enjoy being taught as a change in my retirement'. These answers remind me of the supposed inscription on the tombstone of the Very Tired Housewife:

Don't cry for me now; don't cry for me never;
I'm going to do nothing for ever and ever!

It may be remembered that those of Odysseus' crew who became lotos-eaters bewailed at length (at least in Tennyson's poem) the fact that they had endured slaving at the oars of their master's galley for a very long while:

We have had enough of motion, and of action we
Roll'd to starboard, roll'd to larboard, when the surge was seething free

The very greatest number of replies to the question about not
undertaking convening groups and classes indicated that the
respondents considered themselves too ignorant, too incompetent,
and too diffident to consider doing anything so bold as this. It should
be pointed out that all these replies were given anonymously, so there
was no need to offer excuses to cover up any ulterior reason for not
coming forward, such as laziness. There is no jollying along of
members to be active, and indeed, the lotos-eaters provide a very
positive service to those who wish to be organizers.

WHAT HAS ALL THIS GOT TO DO WITH MEMORY IN LATER LIFE ?
To come back to the question of the preservation memory and
intellectual ability in later life, the lotos-eaters are in rather a
quandary. If they wish to lie back and let the world go by, with no
more mental exertion being demanded of them than watching TV
and consuming easy-to-read paperbacks, they cannot expect to retain
their former mental capacity. It is sad to relate, but I cannot offer
any golden key to memory; as has been reiterated throughout this
book, to retain or develop an adequate memory involves constant
effort, the activity that librarians are continually involved in,
classifying the incoming material and preserving order in the existing
collection.

One of the most common of difficulties in later life is memory for
other people's names. This has been shown by many research
inquiries. Retirement from a job, and of course cessation from all the
work involved in bringing up a family, inevitably means less and less
involvement with other people. In later life your contact with other
people tends to be limited to members of the immediate family and a
few old friends. Organizations such as the U3A, provide a very
valuable service of bringing people together. Although a group may
meet ostensibly to read plays, study philosophy, play bridge, or to

carry out some charitable activity, the most important reason for their meeting may be to retain and develop social contact. I once suggested that a U3A group should be formed with the honest title of 'Gossip', but no one volunteered to convene it – they preferred to give the group some other title when they met for that purpose.

Your interaction with other people may have a far more important effect on your ability to learn and remember than you realize. Social isolation has been shown to produce severe trouble with memory; it leads to conditions of depression giving rise to vicious circle as the following quotation from a depressed sufferer shows:

I feel so low and depressed that everything is just too much effort. I can't even manage very simple jobs without getting distracted or confused, and I just can't concentrate any more ... I'm doing less and less nowadays, and seldom see friends anymore. Whenever I'm out socially I get uncomfortable. People find it difficult to accept me now. It's clear that they either find me boring or embarrassing, so I prefer to avoid these situations.

This sufferer is obviously not a lotos-eater enjoying a quiet retirement from active life – she is miserable and worried by her inefficient memory and inability to concentrate, yet her condition renders her unable to obtain what she needs, social interaction. She would get little benefit from attending a course of memory workshops until her condition of social isolation was remedied.

I shall be dealing with the question of social withdrawal and depression at length in Chapter 8, but mention it here to emphasise that not everyone who is very inactive and takes little part in group activity is like this because they enjoy it or is appreciating a good long rest from their previous labours. By contrast, some individuals withdraw from much social contact for a while because they are immersed in some overwhelmingly absorbing interest of their own, but they are not depressed and suffer from no defect in concentration or memory.

USING STRUCTURED REMINISCENCE
TO CONSOLIDATE YOUR MEMORY

Having reached a good age, and having less need nowadays to be concerned with the day to day grind of earning your living, furthering your business or career, raising the family, etc, you have earned the right to look back and put your past memories into some sort of order, while looking ahead and planning for an enjoyable and worthwhile Third Age. Eric Midwinter, in his stimulating and enjoyable publication *A Voyage of Rediscovery* * urges us to write our life stories! While most of us are not writers, or prepared to launch out into a full auto-biography, the advice he gives is sound as a basis for organizing your past memories into a coherent scheme. If you are concerned about your present and future memory, you should look backwards and review the whole contents of your memory-bank, for as has been emphasised throughout this book, ability to learn and retain new impressions depends upon your being able to relate them to the 'pegs' or 'pigeonholes' that are already well established.

Midwinter justifies his proposal under several headings: 'It might do you good . . . It might help others to understand . . . It might be particularly valuable to your family. . . It might cheer you up.' For purposes of the present book, however, I am concerned that you should create an orderly basis for your future ability to learn and remember. His scheme is interesting in itself, and you may well choose to follow it. He writes:

One approach is, of course, to scribble down everything you can recall over a period of time, and then to reconstitute the material into some kind of shapely product. The material becomes a sort of quarry, from which you take pieces and fashion them to your need. It is rather time consuming, but it does suit some people, and that, to repeat, is the principal point of the exercise. Nonetheless, if you wish to create, either for your own use or for the use of others, a methodical pattern, then

---

* *A Voyage of Rediscovery: a guide to writing your life story*
by Eric Midwinter. Third Age Press, London. 1993. £4.50

you will require some form of synopsis or agenda. Thus the following suggestions, irrespective of whether you begin with a synopsis, may be of value. In the event, many people seem to prefer the 'trigger' quality of a contents column of some kind: it both gets them going and at the same time provides them with a mould for their memories.

He then goes on to list the 'triggers':

A. Culture shocks:

My first day at school.

My first birthday party.

My first holiday and / or trip abroad.

etc.

B. Portmanteau memories:

A typical day when I was about three or four . . . about seven or eight . . . about thirteen . . . at work . . . The same for other aspects of life such as Christmas, summer holiday, weekend, and so forth, finally dealing with such things as a typical year, giving the characteristics at different ages.

C. Cameos:

Here it is suggested that descriptions and profiles are given of members of the extended families, neighbours and local notables, schoolteachers, superiors at work, etc. Locations such as your bedroom, your house, your garden, school, local shops and country-side.

D. Walking with history:

Here it is suggested that past memories should be linked with specially important and memorable national and international events such as the day war broke out. The book has an Appendix which lists about 50 memorable events from 1901 to 1991.

E. My Diary:

Here Midwinter suggests that:

You may feel inclined to move straight ahead to a conventional frame-work. and perhaps the best way of doing that is to conceive the project as a remembered diary, either year by year, or social episode by social episode. It may be that others, having tried one or more of the triggers, and having collected an abundance of fruitful memories, may wish then to re-fashion the material into this more traditional pattern.

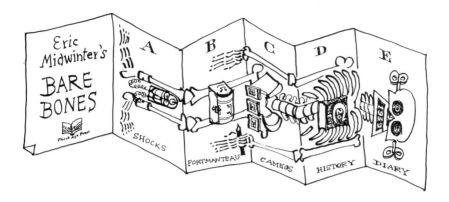

I have simply given the bare bones of Midwinter's scheme above, and have not attempted to convey the richness of all his suggestions which should be read in the original. Although he envisages people in later life setting to and writing some sort of autobiographical account of their lives, I think the majority of people will not attempt anything so ambitious. However, if you are really interested in your memory both now and in the future, I would recommend that you should attempt such an orderly reconstruction of your past life, partly because it is an interesting and worthwhile exercise in itself, and also because it will give you greater insight into how you personally record and store your experience.

    Do not be disappointed if certain periods of your life appear to be quite blank for you at the moment. This is entirely normal and you should not jump to conclusions that some awful mechanism of 'repression' has you in its grip and that you really have 'seen something nasty in the woodshed' that you cannot bear to remember! Some modern psychologists now claim that the whole concept of 'repression' that we have grown up with in the present century is ill conceived, and has the status of a myth. In fact, memories for places, people and incidents that are now inaccessible to you, will be retrieved later on when you have done further work on orderly reminiscence. Give them time! Memory is a reconstructive process that depends upon one cue leading to another.

It is essential to realize that neither you nor anyone else can hope to recall their past lives with complete accuracy, and it does not matter at all. It may be that certain firm memories appear to you as having crystal clarity, and then perhaps you come across old letters, photographs or documents that reveal quite definitely that you were not in that place at that time, or that the colourful dress you remember wearing so well on a certain important occasion was, in fact, worn by your mother! And if your spouse, or old friends remember, quite differently from you, an incident in which you all participated, do not be perturbed. Possibly all of you are wrong in some details – but this is of no great importance. What matters is to construct, over a period of time, a coherent account of your life, and to try to understand why you are now the person you are, and how best you may live the future years of your Third Age.

8

DERANGEMENTS, DISEASES AND INJURIES
THAT AFFECT MEMORY

If you are in reasonable health what is written here need not concern
you, except in so far as you may have friends or members of your
family who have become affected by disease or injury to the brain.
It is included because many people worry in later life. They fear,
quite unnecessarily, that they or their dear ones, are becoming the
victims of 'senile decay'. It seems best to examine the bogy, and to
dismiss it in the vast majority of cases of people who fear that their
memories are failing.

BRAIN DAMAGE
Anyone may have the ill-fortune to be thus affected, and it is
common sense to realize that if the brain is seriously damaged its
functions will be impaired. Injury may occur through a severe crush-
ing of the brain, as in a car accident, the poisoning of the brain by
toxic substances such as lead or excessive alcohol, the breaking of
blood vessels through very high blood pressure, or infection by
bacteria or by virus-like agents that destroy the brain tissue in a
rather mysterious manner.

It should be emphasised that such tragic accidents can happen
at any age; brain damage through injuries are more common in the
younger age groups when people are more exposed to accidents at
work or rushing around in cars and on motorcycles. There are an
estimated 7,500 cases of serious head injury in Britain every year,
with young men the principal victims. Some babies start life with
damaged brains because of accidents at birth, including insufficient
oxygen supplying the brain, and because of their disability they can
never learn normally. In later life there are two main causes of brain
damage: first, the breaking of blood vessels in the brain, and second,

the brain becoming affected by certain diseases. Among the physical changes that come with ageing, the arteries become harder and more brittle, so excessive blood pressure can break them. This may result in a massive haemorrhage (a stroke) which is generally fatal, or leaves the victim impaired to a greater or lesser degree. Alternatively, there may be repeated small breaks that have a cumulative effect, and are eventually fatal. The second main cause is through diseases of the Alzheimer type: the brain tissue becomes slowly destroyed as though by a virus infection, and as yet the precise nature of the infection or degeneration has not been established.

SO-CALLED 'SENILE DECAY'

The term 'senile decay' is seldom used today because in pre-scientific medicine it was assumed that the mere fact of ageing caused decay of the brain, an assumption that was quite erroneous. When people's behaviour alters and they appear to be 'losing their memory' it is very dangerous to assume that they are suffering from some form of 'senile decay' as the following case illustrates.

An active old man in his mid-80s alarmed his family by appearing to change very markedly. He sat in his chair and no longer showed interest in food or his usual concerns. Three times he had parked his car, forgotten where he had parked it, and reported it stolen. Eventually the police became fed up and suggested that he had outlived his eligibility for a licence. On examination he was rational but a little confused, and a local G.P. diagnosed 'old age'.

The old man's son was a well-known doctor specializing in geriatric medicine, and the family reported to him that 'Dad was failing'. The son investigated the case and found that his father was perfectly fit physically, but following the death of his second wife he suffered badly from insomnia, so he had been taking sleeping tablets, and the drug had reduced him to this condition that resembled the so-called 'senile decay'. This medication was stopped, and within ten days the old man was back to his vigorous and very active self.

This case is fairly typical of what may happen in later life if people resort habitually to medically prescribed drugs that are intended to make them sleep and calm them down, and perhaps over-use them. People react to drugs in individual ways, and their reactions change as they age.

Over-use of drugs is not the only cause of apparent 'senile decay' – food supplements such as some vitamins can cause trouble if taken in grossly excessive quantities as the following case illustrates.

A lady of 79 was brought to hospital by her daughter because she had ceased to eat, or talk to anyone, and appeared to be demented. During her stay in hospital, during which nothing much wrong could be discovered in her physical condition, her mental condition improved and she returned to normal, and was discharged. It was then discovered by questioning the daughter that this lady had been taking vitamin tablets of a proprietary brand that were nicely coated with chocolate, and as she liked the flavour she had been consuming about 50 a day! This massive dose of vitamin D had had a disastrous effect on her and she had sunk into a condition resembling dementia.

HYSTERICAL AMNESIA

Is grandad just shamming? You have probably heard of 'hysterical' conditions, and extraordinary cases of people who have apparently 'lost their memories' and wander away from home, apparently unaware of who they are. Such cases are very rare indeed – more common are episodes in which a person appears suddenly to have lost her or his memory, fails to recognize old friends and members of the family, and claims not to know such ordinary things as the time of year or where they are living. These episodes are generally diagnosed as 'hysterical' or 'psychogenic' amnesia; they appear to take place when the sufferer is confronted with conditions that cause great anxiety, problems that are, perhaps, quite unknown to the family.

Typically, these episodes are of quite limited duration: a week or so or even a month or two. Memory comes back when the anxiety-provoking situation has been somehow resolved. As with all hysterical conditions, there is generally a suspicion that a certain amount of shamming is involved, the amnesia not being as profound as it appears. It may be that the hysteric does not wish to remember, in order to escape from a very difficult situation, often connected with marital discord, guilt over financial problems, or some shameful happening that engenders fear of reprisals from some quarter. When the hysterical episode is over, the sufferer typically shrugs off questions about the period during which he had lost his memory with evasive replies such as, 'Oh I have always had a terribly bad memory', and tries to make light of the incident that was very worrying for other people.

This kind of transient hysterical amnesia can occur at any age although it is rather more common in younger people. Someone has described it as, 'a weak attempt by a weak personality to escape conflicts which are chiefly conflicts of actual life.' The sort of person who is subject to these attacks (and they may occur repeatedly) goes through life attempting to evade responsibility, and is never quite honest with himself or with other people. Freudians say that hysterical amnesia typifies the mechanism of repression: the events are not remembered because of the anxiety they would arouse.

TRANSIENT GLOBAL AMNESIA

Accounts of cases of hysterical amnesia used to appear in the medical press quite frequently up to the 1950s, and then they became quite infrequent. To some extent they were replaced by reports of another form of transient amnesia known as TGA or Transient Global Amnesia, a condition that was first clearly described by a number of doctors in the 1950s. It seems likely that earlier on it had been confused with hysterical amnesia, but the two conditions are very different.

TGA occurs in middle aged or elderly people (very few cases occur before the age of 40) and affects men and women of quite normal personality who are in quite good health. Its onset is dramatically sudden and the sufferer's family may often assume that it is the result of a stroke, and that their relative will be disabled for life.

The outstanding feature of it is that those afflicted keep asking questions such as, 'Where am I?', 'What's happening?', 'What time of day is it?', 'Am I ill?' But although the questions are answered, they are constantly repeated again and again, because the normal mechanism of processing what is in the short-term memory has ceased to function. This characteristic question asking is in contrast to the hysteric amnesiac who does not ask questions, and although confused, does not wish to be confronted with information. As well as being unable to remember any new material, the TGA victim has amnesia for the more immediate past, but again in contrast to the hysteric, there is no loss of personal identity.

The shocked family soon have their anxiety relieved in cases of TGA, for the condition soon clears up spontaneously. Typically, it lasts from between eight to 24 hours, and then the normal processes of memory begin to return and, surprisingly enough, the victim seems no worse for this extraordinary experience for normality is completely restored. There is a complete blackout of memory for the whole episode.

What causes this dramatic transient disruption of the whole memory process, which may happen to anyone in later life even though they may be of normal personality and apparently in good health? Although it has been studied for over 30 years, no one really knows. Unlike hysterical amnesia, there is no evidence that it is the result of an emotional conflict, and it is fairly certain that it is caused by physical events within the brain. Sometimes it is prefaced by a stressful experience such as swimming in very cold water, or physical exhaustion through heavy work. In some cases the stress may be emotional, such as the shock of hearing bad news, but often there may be no preceding stress, the attack coming out of the blue.

Those studying TGA have advanced three main theories about its occurrence, linking it with migraine, or disease of the arteries, or with epilepsy, but none of these theories has obtained general acceptance. Fortunately it seldom recurs, and attacks are generally one-off incidents. It is not a common disorder, but a predisposition to it appears to run in families, and it remains one of the great mysteries for those who are studying memory. It is difficult to estimate its frequency; because it is soon over people may not report it to their doctors. Grandad is certainly not shamming if he has an attack of TGA!

SO-CALLED 'SENILE DEMENTIA'

Has grandad lost his mind for good? A book on Senile Dementia begins with a cartoon showing two figures who are presumably social workers, and one of them is saying to the other, 'Senile dementia? Isn't that when elderly clients disagree with you about what's best for them?' This pretty well illustrates the common over-use of the term 'dementia.'

The question, 'Has grandad lost his mind for good?' is not easily answered. If it is a confirmed case of disease of the Alzheimer type there is really no hope of improvement, but if you find that an elderly relative is very unhappy, confused and apparently unable to remember anything, sometimes this is a case of 'pseudo-dementia'. He seems to be in the condition of someone who is the victim of a degenerative disease who will soon need hospitalization or constant supervision from a carer, but this may be a mistaken diagnosis, and with appropriate treatment he may recover completely. There are some significant differences between the condition of real dementia and pseudo-dementia. In the former, sufferers typically try to cover up loss of memory and disorientation by bland answers, and they pretend to be more normal than they are. In the latter condition, there is a distinct tendency to exaggerate disability and to claim that they are quite incapable of looking after themselves.

Pseudo-dementia is a form of hysterical disorder, such as I discussed earlier, but it is not an episode that will pass away once a crisis is over; it may become a permanent condition. It is likely that in the hospital wards that house demented patients suffering from diseases of the Alzheimer type, there are some patients who have nothing wrong with their brains, but are cases of pseudo-dementia that could be rehabilitated if sufficient trouble, time and expense were devoted to their sad individual cases. It is also likely that the two conditions may occur together, a very mildly dementing patient appearing to be much worse because of the sad social conditions involved, and the consequent psychological attitude.

It may seem strange that some people should wish to be thought worse than they are, and say that they just can't remember anything or be responsible for their actions, when such a presentation of themselves generally results in their being housed and cared for in the most dreary settings and being treated like a helpless child, but this condition is not the result of a rational decision to become dependent on others; it is frequently caused by a major depressive breakdown.

DEPRESSION

At any stage of life depressive illness will prevent people from functioning normally. They become hopelessly forgetful and incapable of making rational decisions, and if the depression comes in later life they may assume that they are really suffering from some horrid degenerative disease, and this suspicion, however unwarranted, may make them even more depressed. Depression often follows the experience of being bereaved in later life, and bereaved

people (especially men) frequently go through a period of mourning during which the death rate from various causes, including suicide, is significantly raised. They just stop looking after themselves.

The old idea of treating depressed people with brisk and unsympathetic injunctions to 'pull themselves together' unfortunately does not have the intended effect. Depression is an illness, and like other serious illnesses it requires specialist treatment. Fortunately it is curable, and so the sufferers can regain a normal ability to learn, remember and look after themselves.

The acutely depressed person is obviously unwell, and recognizes that he or she is undergoing an illness which needs treatment. There are also milder forms of depression which may consist simply of a dreary loss of enjoyment of life, with a lack of initiative to do anything. These conditions may go on intermittently for quite a long time. If the sufferer is elderly it may seem that this is the natural result of growing old and we can't do much about it.

Can't we just!

Such a state of mind may be, in some cases, the result of the totally negative stereotype of ageing that is prevalent in our youth-orientated culture. There is no reason at all why older people should be made to devalue themselves. Their lives are as important as anyone else's and recovery from mild depression involves rebellion against the forces in society that would relegate them to the position of second-class citizens. Ceasing to take pleasure in life, insomnia, loss of appetite, disinterest in sex, are not the natural results of ageing; they are largely caused by a negative attitude, and the many unfair and preventable things that older people are expected to put up with in our society.

It is no wonder that some older people appear to be stupid, incompetent, dull as ditchwater, demented – it is not because their wits have decayed and their brains are like shrivelled walnuts, as so many people believe, but because they are depressed – horribly, drearily depressed. It is not the major sort of melancholia that requires anti-depressant drugs or hospital treatment; it is a nasty, sinister form of depression, which many people think of as just being 'old age'.

Depression affects memory, both at the stage of encoding new material and retrieval. A large amount of the supposed deterioration of memory with age is simply due to the apathy that is a major feature of this condition. Being to some degree apathetic, depressed people cannot summon up the energy to work on the contents of the short-term memory and encode it efficiently in the memory-bank. The same apathy prevents them from putting any effort into the process of retrieving the information they already possess.

Recovery from this sort of depression, which looks as though it were a deterioration of the wits, involves the development of a new attitude to life on the part of the sufferer. Fortunately there are encouraging signs that the present generations of older people are not prepared to put up with the dreary sort of life that was the expected lot of their parents. They don't wear a special sort of clothes like a uniform of those who are 'past it', but vie with their daughters and sons in wearing attractive clothes. They are not afraid to treat themselves to interesting holidays abroad. They are joining organizations such as the University of the Third Age that cater for all sorts of interests. The older generation are in revolt.

'SENILITY' THE NON-EXISTENT DISEASE

Are you becoming 'senile' yourself? What does the term 'senile' mean? According to the Oxford English Dictionary the original meaning was 'Belonging to, suited for, or incident to old age', so if I am a man of 80 (which presumably is in 'old age') my behaviour and capacities should rightly be 'senile', as befits a 'Senior Citizen'. But the dictionary goes on to say, Now only of diseases, etc, peculiar to the aged' so a change has taken place in our language, and to be 'senile' is to be 'diseased'. This is how the term is commonly used. It indicates the widespread assumption that we will all lose our wits if we live long enough.

If, when in your 30s, you had a bad attack of influenza and found yourself very forgetful and unable to concentrate or think clearly, you blamed the condition of 'flu. But if you succumb to the same infection when in your 70s you are likely to blame your age for your mental condition. It is difficult to throw off the traditional assumption that age in itself is some sort of illness, whereas in reality the only relevance that age has to psychological incapacity is that you are less robust when you are older, and hence more likely to be knocked up by illnesses.

Now that there are many more people in the older section of the population than there used to be, doctors are waking up to the fact that they don't know much about how illness affects people in later life. They go on applying the methods that are appropriate to young and middle-aged adults, and you can't blame them for this, for they have had little experience in dealing with older people either in their training or their practice, but they are beginning to realize that it is inappropriate to hand out tranquillizers and sleeping pills that have their uses in the transient disorders of younger people.

Alex Comfort, a very distinguished doctor and specialist in geriatric medicine, began a lecture as follows:

I want to talk to you about a non-existent disease. 'Senility' is the gradual loss of mental and physical function and well-being when this occurs in an elderly person. Its distinction from general ill health depends upon the erroneous belief that age in itself is a sufficient explanation for such changes.

So the proper answer to the question 'Are you becoming senile ?', in terms of most modern medical thinking is 'No', because you cannot suffer from a non-existent disease! You can suffer from ill health, yes, and such ill-health may cause difficulty in learning, incidents of forgetfulness, lack of concentration and other psychological problems, but it is hardly sensible to blame them on your age, however old you are. Periods of forgetfulness, etc, that are due to physical conditions such as myxoedema (lack of thyroid hormone), diabetes, urinary infections, etc, must be sharply distinguished from the forgetfulness that is due to a diseased or injured brain. The former type of ailments can be treated and the sufferer regain normal intellectual function, but a damaged brain cannot be repaired to restore it to full function.

DISEASES OF THE ALZHEIMER TYPE

Diseases of the Alzheimer type that actually destroy brain tissue, and progressively obliterate the power to learn and remember, have recently come into public awareness because of the publicity given to the 'mad cow disease' which resembles some brain diseases that affect humans. There is a lot of controversy as to whether we shall be perfectly safe in eating the muscular tissue of beef, but refrain from eating the brains or neural tissue.

I only mention this controversy here to emphasise that you should not confuse the changes in memory that take place in normal ageing with the pathological changes that result from brains being destroyed by viruses, spirochaetes, and other horrid organisms. No doubt a similar controversy is in progress among the cannibal tribes of New Guinea where they suffer from kuru, a disease that has much the same effect as Alzheimer's. Cannibals contract it through eating the brains of victims who have the disease, but it is said that if they confined themselves to eating just the fleshy parts of their victim, they would be safe.

THE RISKS OF AGEING

What are your chances of losing your wits ? The longer you live the longer you are at risk from all sorts of accidents happening to you, even such improbable accidents as being struck by lightning. We are all equally at risk but it is natural that you should wonder just what are the chances of your becoming such a victim.

It is not easy to give any precise figure of probability. At present, Alzheimer's disease accounts for over 50% of dementias occurring over the age of 65, and some statistics show that about 10% of the population over that age succumb to it. I am not directly concerned with medical problems – this book is about the memory of normal, healthy people in later life, and the problems that they encounter. Much depends upon what age you are now. Alzheimer's disease may have a genetic component, although the fact that someone in your family has died of it does not mean that you are very likely to develop it. There are cases in which one identical twin developed it and the other did not. It seems more likely that the possession of a particular gene is necessary for you to be susceptible to it. Suppose we say that you are programmed by your genetic constitution to be a type susceptible to Alzheimer's disease in your mid-80s – you may never succumb to it, first because being susceptible to something does not mean that you will ever develop it, and second, because you may be run over by a bus on your 80th birthday. The longer you live, the more at risk you will be for all sorts of things happening to you, but the longer you live the more you will benefit from the considerable progress medical science is making in research directed to eliminating these nasty diseases. One expert in geriatric medicine, writing seven years ago, gave it as his opinion that:

For the future the research outlook is bright – replacement of the chemical messengers which are lost in Alzheimer, use of protective and palliative drugs, and discovery of the cause or causes are all on the agenda of the next 10 or 20 years. Your best insurance is to see that the work is funded, not made the subject of politically motivated cuts because 'the old don't matter.'

INDEX

Third Age Press

The Third Age Press recognises that the period of life after full-time, gainful employment and family responsibility can be a time of fulfilment and continuing personal development . . . a time of regeneration.

We hope that our publications will also give pleasure and lead the users into many rewarding pursuits

Lifelines

is a series of publications focusing on the presentation of your own life. They seek to stimulate reflection . . . to see the lines that connect your life not only with the past, but to the present and the future as well.

A VOYAGE OF REDISCOVERY:
a guide to writing your life story
For individuals or groups wanting to reflect on their lives but not quite sure how to start. Incudes a 20th Century date list to help you place yourself in history.
By Eric Midwinter   £4.50

•••

LIFELINES **TITLES** AVAILABLE

ENCORE: a guide to planning a celebration of your life
Every life deserves an 'encore' and this book has been written
to encourage you to set out the ways in which you would like to
be remembered . . . or, use it as a novel parlour game. £2.50
• • •
THE RHUBARB PEOPLE: Eric Midwinter's Voyage of Rediscovery
In case you need an example of how to set out on your voyage, the
author of the two books above offers his own witty and poignant
adventures of growing up in Manchester of the 30s. £4.50
• •
THE RHUBARB PEOPLE is also available on a 90 minute audio-
cassette recorded by the author and including some suggestions
about writing or recording your own life story £7.00
• • •
IN THE **Lifelines** SERIES – SUMMER 1995
GETTING TO KNOW ME is aimed at family members and
carers who want to record, not only the lives of older people, but
also some of the practical information needed to make the caring of
old people a richer time for both parties.
• • •
And
Lifescapes which describes and illustrates how to create a
unique pictorial representation of your , or someone else's life.
A **Lifescape** is a collage of pictures and mementoes which will
appeal to young and old working together – either as a reminiscence
project or a way to create and make a very special heirloom.
• • •
All prices, here and overleaf, include p & p. from:
Third Age Press,
6 Parkside Gardens, London SW19 5EY

Third Age Press

THE PLAY READER:
Seven Dramas by Thirdagers

This collection of seven one-act plays is the result of a competition open to older people. The plays are ideal for reading in groups or rehearsed readings and are equally suited for performance. Their rich variety is certain to challenge and stimulate discussion as well as provide entertainment.

Just Us: a two handed psychological drama

The Confession: a mystery set in 19th Century Paris

Twenty – Forty: the Third Age of the future

Other Ways: a drama set in a tour group on holiday in Greece

This is My Son: a child of a wartime romance reunited with its mother

Pax Pacata: set in Roman Britain with an all woman cast

Mellow: a comedy duet for two women

Cast lists range from a two hander
to a troupe of seven

• • •

£6.50 or £5.00 each for five or more copies.
Performance rights are detailed in the book.

• • •

perspectives

*The **Perspectives** series was launched to meet the needs of people who, having written their life stories, wanted to preserve them, either for themselves, their family, or a wider public.*

• • •

CHILD OF THE WAR: An Evacuee in Devon

Wally Harbert's vivid account of one child's experience evokes traditional farm life as well as the exhilaration and the fear in London during the War.   £7.10

• • •

All prices include p & p.

Cheques to **Third Age Press** please

6 Parkside Gardens, London SW19 5EY

Third Age Press

The University of the Third Age

has local groups throughout the UK

For information about your nearest U3A

please send a sae to

U3A

1 Stockwell Green, London SW9 9JF